WOMEN IN CHURCH HISTORY

Also by Joanne Turpin:

Catholic Traditions: Treasures New and Old
Twelve Apostolic Women
The World of Jesus: Culture, History, Religion, Politics, Geography

WOMEN IN CHURCH HISTORY

21 STORIES FOR 21 CENTURIES

JOANNE TURPIN

ST. ANTHONY MESSENGER PRESS
Cincinnati, Ohio

Scripture citations are taken from the *New Revised Standard Version Bible*,
copyright ©1989 by the Division of Christian Education of the National
Council of the Churches of Christ in the U.S.A., and are used by permission.
All rights reserved.

Cover and book design by Mark Sullivan
Cover image ©istockphoto.com/ Simon Oxley

LIBRARY OF CONGRESS CATALOGING-IN-PUBLICATION DATA

Turpin, Joanne.
Women in church history : 21 stories for 21 centuries / Joanne Turpin.
p. cm.
Includes bibliographical references.
ISBN-13: 978-0-86716-776-4 (pbk. : alk. paper) 1. Catholic women—Biography.
2. Catholics—Biography. 3. Christian women—Biography. 4. Christian biography. I. Title.

BX4667.T87 2007
270.092′2—dc22
[B]
2006030480

ISBN 978-0-86716-776-4
Copyright ©1990, 2007, Joanne Turpin. All rights reserved.

Published by St. Anthony Messenger Press
28 W. Liberty St.
Cincinnati, OH 45202
www.AmericanCatholic.org

Printed in the United States of America.

Printed on acid-free paper.

For my daughters,
Patricia and Sharon Turpin

CONTENTS

INTRODUCTION | 1

THE FIRST CENTURY: PRISCA THE EVANGELIST | 5

THE SECOND CENTURY: PERPETUA OF CARTHAGE | 16

THE THIRD CENTURY: APOLLONIA OF ALEXANDRIA | 25

THE FOURTH CENTURY: MACRINA OF CAPPADOCIA | 33

THE FIFTH CENTURY: PULCHERIA OF CONSTANTINOPLE | 42

THE SIXTH CENTURY: BRIGID OF KILDARE | 51

THE SEVENTH CENTURY: HILDA OF WHITBY | 61

THE EIGHTH CENTURY: LIOBA, ANGLO-SAXON MISSIONARY TO GERMANY | 70

THE NINTH CENTURY: LUDMILA OF BOHEMIA | 79

THE TENTH CENTURY: ADELAIDE, EMPRESS OF THE HOLY ROMAN EMPIRE | 87

THE ELEVENTH CENTURY: MARGARET OF SCOTLAND | 96

THE TWELFTH CENTURY: HILDEGARD OF BINGEN | 105

THE THIRTEENTH CENTURY: CLARE OF ASSISI | 116

THE FOURTEENTH CENTURY: CATHERINE OF SIENA | 128

THE FIFTEENTH CENTURY: CATHERINE OF GENOA | 139

THE SIXTEENTH CENTURY: TERESA OF AVILA | 149

THE SEVENTEENTH CENTURY: LOUISE DE MARILLAC | 160

THE EIGHTEENTH CENTURY: ANNE MARIE JAVOUHEY | 170

THE NINETEENTH CENTURY: ELIZABETH LANGE | 181

THE TWENTIETH CENTURY: JEAN DONOVAN | 192

THE TWENTY-FIRST CENTURY: DOROTHY STANG | 203

CONCLUSION | 214

SELECTED BIBLIOGRAPHY | 215

NOTES | 218

INDEX | 223

INTRODUCTION

Jesus made no secret about his feelings toward women. He gifted them with his healing touch, invited them to be among his disciples and welcomed them as friends. In turn, they supported his mission, followed him along the dark road to Calvary and remained faithfully near the tomb. Jesus rewarded their fidelity with the supreme joy of being the first witnesses to his Resurrection. That's where the story of women in the church begins—and a glorious beginning it is.

If in subsequent centuries historians tended to focus on his-story to the neglect of her-story, blame it on the way they approach their subject. The past has traditionally been described in terms of power struggles, battles of various types—actions and events typically engaged in by men. Such reporting is as typical of church history as of the secular kind.

Yet, as Brazilian theologian Leonardo Boff observes: "Strong, independent, decisive women have never been lacking in the history of the Church to show forth the feminine in its true qualities." After mentioning a few names, he goes on to say, "These and countless other women, towers of strength, stand as rays of hope...."[1] If one combs the "Acts of the Martyrs," the lives of the saints, diaries and biographies written long ago, her-story begins to fall into place.

This book presents twenty-one women, famous and obscure, each painted against the backdrop of the church in her century. They were chosen to represent her-story in twenty-one centuries of church history according to three criteria: personal holiness, moral courage and the importance of the individual's contribution to the immediate or long-range course of the pilgrim church.

One of the happier discoveries comes from finding that Jesus (if one may put him in the same category as Christian males) had much company in supporting and encouraging women to use the gifts God gave them and in working in partnership with them. The apostle Paul appears on this list and so do Boniface and Francis of Assisi and Vincent de Paul and a host of others. Of course, it was to their benefit!

In the following pages, women serve as missionaries and martyrs, reformers and peacemakers, pioneers and prophets, teachers and humanitarians, mystics and writers of spiritual literature. They prove that living the gospel can be done in varied ways, responding to the particular needs of the time and circumstances of life. Once they heard a call from God, nothing—neither official opposition nor family pressure nor even, in some cases, poor health—prevented them from saying yes. They were willing to risk censure, humiliation, even death, in order to answer the call.

From the research into their lives, two messages come across rather vividly.

First, each understood the true meaning of love. This was clearly the motivating force for all: love for the Lord spilling out to encompass humanity. Teresa of Avila perhaps expressed it best: "O my Jesus, how much a soul can do when ablaze with Thy love!"[2]

The power of such love makes an even greater impression when one realizes that society through most of these centuries did not exactly push women to the fore. Nevertheless, with the Lord on their side, how could they go wrong? Sometimes it just took longer for them to make their point.

A second message these stories give is an emphasis on service, loving service. As an illustration of this, beyond the predictable ways suggested by the term, is the surprising incidence of women washing the feet of others as an act of humble service in imitation of Jesus at the Last Supper. "For I have set you an example," he said to his disciples then, "that you also should do as I have done to you" (John 13:15). The women take Jesus literally, doing this in memory of him. They did not regard foot-washing as an act to be reserved as symbolic ritual for a Holy Week liturgy.

Taking Jesus' words to heart has turned ordinary Christians into extraordinary Christians—women as well as men. There's a lesson in that for all of us.

THE FIRST CENTURY

PRISCA THE EVANGELIST

BACKGROUND

The Acts of the Apostles vividly describes the first Pentecost. Crowds of Jewish pilgrims had come to Jerusalem for the sacred Feast of Weeks, originally a harvest festival. There they heard Peter preach the Good News—and a rich harvest it turned out to be in terms of converts to faith in Jesus Christ. The converted pilgrims returned to their homes in provinces scattered throughout the Roman Empire to share the exciting news with their Jewish brothers and sisters in diaspora, that is, outside Palestine. (More Jews lived outside biblical Palestine than within its borders at the time.)

Persecution also played a significant role in spreading the faith. When Jewish authorities attempted to stamp out the new sect through persecution, many Christianized Jews sought refuge in Antioch, a city several hundred miles north of Jerusalem. Antioch was where the name "Christian" was first applied to followers of Jesus Christ and also where the conversion of Gentiles in a largely pagan population began in earnest.

In Antioch the apostle Paul—after his own dramatic conversion —joined with Barnabas, a leader in the church, to preach the message of salvation through faith in Jesus. Their missionary endeavors eventually took them to the nearby island of Cyprus. Later would come travels to other provinces of Asia Minor and, scarcely a dozen years after Jesus' crucifixion, to the European continent.

Other missionaries included John Mark who, according to tradition, authored the second Gospel. His mother Mary, one of the early disciples, had opened her home in Jerusalem to fellow believers. This likely was the first house church, Christians meeting and worshiping together. As Acts 12:12 relates, when Peter was miraculously freed from imprisonment, "he went to the house of Mary, the mother of John whose other name was Mark, where many had gathered and were praying."

Within decades, Mary's house church was to be duplicated in communities across the Middle East and Europe.

CORINTH, AD 50

In this noisy, thriving maritime city forty miles southwest of Athens, a couple from Rome finds refuge. Prisca and her husband Aquila are among a group of people expelled from the capital by edict of the Emperor Claudius. He sought by his action to restore public order after a series of sectarian disturbances in certain quarters of the city where synagogues were located. The trouble rages over a man called "Chrestus."

Prisca, a woman of aristocratic background, is believed to be related to the family of Pudens, a well-known Roman senator. According to talk, the entire Pudens household has been converted to a new sect known as Christianity, which originated in the East. Aquila's status as a freeperson means that, though once a slave, he won freedom either by purchasing it or working for it. Marriage of an ex-slave into a family like Prisca's is not uncommon among Romans.

Nobility of birth does not keep Prisca from helping her husband earn a living. The two waste no time in setting up a business in the agora, or marketplace, of Corinth. Aquila, a tent-maker by trade, weaves or repairs items such as tents, ships' sails and the awnings used over shops.

Corinth offers ample opportunity for trade, situated as the city is on an isthmus linking northern and southern Greece. It also boasts two seaports, one on either side of the isthmus, making Corinth's agora a crossroads of humanity: bankers and sailors, artisans and government officials, philosophers and fortune-tellers.

In the midst of this highly mobile society—and a pagan one at that—Prisca and Aquila not only set up shop but also organize a church in their house like the one they had in Rome. For the two are followers of "the Way" of Jesus Christ and, whenever they find others who share the belief, they invite them to join the community meeting in their home. The couple extends this invitation to their business contacts too, given the chance to steer conversation into more philosophical channels and to explain what Christ's teachings have meant in their own lives.

Christians, as these believers are often called, tend to be viewed with suspicion since their lifestyle contrasts so sharply with that of the pagan majority. More typical Corinthians take advantage of the diversions—violent gladiator contests, for example, or obscene theatrical performances—that keep them from thinking too deeply about the essential emptiness of their lives. Pagan religion offers little to counteract this poverty of spirit, notwithstanding all the architecturally beautiful temples in and around the agora. Inescapably, greatest attention goes to the temple honoring Aphrodite, goddess of love, which stands on the heights of Acrocorinth, a mountaintop acropolis looming more than eighteen hundred feet above the city. From the summit, on a clear day, one can see the gleaming temples atop the acropolis in Athens.

For Prisca and Aquila, however, there is little time for gazing afar. After a busy day at the tent-making trade, they spend evenings instructing people more deeply in the faith. Corinthians are a lively lot who sometimes misplace their enthusiasm; special care must be taken to give them a solid, sober grounding in gospel teachings.

At least once a week the little community of believers gathers to celebrate the Lord's Supper: a sacramental breaking of bread and blessing of the cup performed by whomever is designated to preside at the meal. The sacred meal memorializes Jesus' sharing of bread and wine with his disciples at the Last Supper. Along with this sacramental act, the membership reads from scrolls of the Law and the prophets of Hebrew Scripture—for their faith has its roots in Jewish tradition. Treasured sayings of Jesus are recalled as well, followed by one in the group preaching on the Word. The worship service includes prayers and hymn-singing.

At some time during the accompanying table fellowship (which was a marked feature of Jesus' ministry), they talk of the news from other similar communities scattered about the provinces of the empire. House churches stay amazingly well-informed about each other's activities, for letters can be easily carried by Christian business or missionary travelers going via the expansive network of Roman roads.

Not long after Prisca and Aquila settle in Corinth, news comes in a form even more welcome than letters: this time in the person of Paul, a noted and—as they have heard—often controversial evangelist.

When he arrives from a disappointing sojourn in Athens, Paul goes directly to the street of tent-makers in the agora, for finding work in his own trade to support himself is a priority to him. Here he makes acquaintance with the couple from Rome, and they immediately invite him to work at the shop and to lodge at their home. For the next eighteen months this close association continues until missionary work calls all of them to another city.

Prisca and Aquila also put Paul in touch with the local synagogue, for he had yet to give up on the idea of convincing his Jewish brothers and sisters that "the Way" is a fulfillment, not a contradiction, of Judaism. Prisca and Aquila think along the same lines, as do many who have committed their lives to following Jesus and continue to attend synagogue services. There one finds not just Jews but also Gentiles (called "God-fearers") attracted to belief in one God as expressed by Judaism.

While Aquila avoids confrontation with his fellow Jews, concentrating his energies instead on guidance of house church members, Paul, who is outspoken by temperament, quickly runs into opposition. As elsewhere, Paul's zeal will eventually lead to trouble.

For her part, Prisca, though educated and willing enough to speak wherever she can get a hearing, knows better than even to consider raising her voice at the synagogue gathering. Women there are not allowed a participatory role, let alone permitted to sit alongside their husbands. (Although a few scholars have disputed this, the limited evidence they offer thus far comes several centuries later, and applies only to certain areas.) Only men are counted in determining if the requisite number to conduct a service are present.

After a traditional synagogue service on the Sabbath, members of the Christian sect on the next day keep special the Lord's Day. Prisca surely appreciates all the more the egalitarian atmosphere of the house church. For female followers of Christ may pray and prophesy during the service when so moved and preside over the sacred meal, too. (This, in fact, becomes a necessity in communities where women alone constitute the original congregation. Surely that was the case after Paul baptized Lydia and the other women at Philippi—his first converts on European soil.)

As is bound to happen, members occasionally raise the issue of women's visible role or complain at having to share the customary fellowship meal with the mixed social classes typical of a house church. Paul then likes to remind them of a special blessing of their faith, something he put into writing in a letter addressed to the Galatians: "There is no longer Jew or Greek, there is no longer slave or free, there is no longer male and female; for all of you are one in Christ Jesus" (3:28).

Prisca sees clear evidence of his fair-mindedness not just in the way Paul treats her as a coworker, but also in the regard and confidence he places in Phoebe, patroness of a group that meets in her house in the nearby port of Cenchreae, only a three-hour walk away.

In the spring of AD 51 everyone looks forward to the popular Isthmian Games, due again in Corinth in April and May. The festival of athletic events and other entertainment, held every two years in honor of Poseidon (god of the sea), draws scores of tourists. With inns limited in number and of poor quality besides, tents are needed to house visitors in the plains surrounding the walled city. This translates into booming business for tentmakers as well as an ideal opportunity to spread the Good News among customers.

Trouble for Paul and his coworkers comes afterward, not for evangelizing the festival's visitors but, rather, for succeeding too well in making converts from among the local population–people the synagogue claims. Jewish leaders zero in on Paul, attempting through court action to get the provincial authority to restrain the man. But the proconsul, Rome's representative in Corinth, refuses to interfere, instead dismissing the case.

At some point after these legal proceedings, the decision is made to move on, for fresh missionary fields beckon. Paul's stay in Corinth actually has been longer than is his habit. When he selects Ephesus, one of the great cities of the empire, as the next destination, there seems to be no question about his friends and coworkers, Prisca and Aquila, going along too. Since ship movement essentially ceases during the winter months, however, it is not until the spring of AD 52 that they depart.

The leisurely ten-day voyage across the Aegean Sea takes them past island scenery of breathtaking beauty. Near the southwest coast of Asia Minor mountains appear through a blue haze, and soon the missionaries are sailing into the inner harbor of Ephesus. Boasting one of the Seven Wonders of the World, the temple of Artemis (goddess of fertility), the city spreads itself out in the foreground of a natural amphitheater.

While Aquila sets up shop in the agora and Prisca readies their newest home to accommodate meetings of Christians already living in Ephesus, Paul spends a brief period trying to woo members of the local synagogue, but with little success. Knowing he leaves the house church in capable hands, Paul goes on to Jerusalem, then visits Antioch and other congregations in Asia Minor that he had founded at an earlier date.

In Ephesus Prisca keeps busy not only preaching the gospel but also looking for ways to provide support and sustenance for the poorer members of her community, especially the widows.

(In the society of that day, widows often had few resources of their own.) Another condition for females that appalls Prisca is the temple-associated prostitution carried on by young women designated as priestesses—a common practice in cities of the East.

Paul is still away on his travels when Apollos of Alexandria comes to town. An authority on Scripture, he delivers a brilliant commentary at the synagogue, holding his listeners spellbound. But when he turns to discoursing on the Way of the Lord, Prisca and Aquila, who are present, find his knowledge of Jesus incomplete and on many points incorrect. After the service they take Apollos home so that Prisca can instruct him properly.

Apollos accepts with good grace the corrections of this obviously educated woman. Moreover, he learns that she hails from the Christian community of Rome. A decade earlier it had hosted a visit from the apostle Peter and his wife, who faithfully passed on the teachings of Jesus and explained in detail how he had fulfilled the biblical prophesy of the Messiah.

By the time Paul returns to Ephesus, Apollos, armed with new knowledge, has journeyed on to Corinth to see how he might fare among its Jews.

The Corinthians are next heard from when emissaries deliver a message from Chloe, the woman in whose home the Christians now meet. Problems have surfaced that require expert advice. What reminiscences Paul and his companions must have had before he began dictating his First Letter to the Corinthians, with its elevating words on the need for love along with down-to-earth admonitions concerning unseemly behavior at the Lord's Supper.

In Ephesus the conduct of Christians causes trouble, too, but trouble of a different type. Having earlier witnessed for their faith by publicly burning expensive scrolls of magic formulas (the city being a world center for the magic arts), the Christians next wage a campaign against a vital product of the silversmith trade: stat-ues of Artemis.

Spring approaches, and with it comes the start of another pil-grimage season when many thousands of devotees of the goddess Artemis converge upon the city. The fervor of pilgrims streaming in from all parts of the empire to visit the temple-shrine is matched by the zeal of local silversmiths who make souvenirs: both replicas of the shrine and silver statuettes of Artemis. The latter—depictions of a many-breasted goddess—prove particularly offensive to Christians. But for the silversmiths, the statuette rep-resents their great moneymaker for the year.

When a leading silversmith, Demetrius by name, hears Christians preach against the manufacture of these souvenirs—labeling them idolatrous—he organizes his own protest group made up of fellow artisans. Pilgrims join in the ensuing uproar. Paul and his friends become targets when a near riot takes place at the city's vast open-air theater, though a public official finally manages to cool the high-pitched emotions of the mob.

About the time that order is restored to Ephesus, word comes that Rome has a new emperor. Rumor runs rampant that the pre-vious emperor, Claudius, has been poisoned by his fourth wife. Now, in AD 54, her son by a former marriage, Nero, has assumed the throne. It's just the kind of gossip to capture the public fancy. The silversmith episode thus becomes old news.

Since Nero's record contains no opposition to Christianity, Prisca and Aquila feel safe to return to Rome to their house church on the Aventine Hill, where they will renew acquaintance with old friends and family.

That the couple does resume their role as congregational leaders in the seat of the empire is evident from a letter Paul writes later to the house churches in Rome (the number having grown to some half-dozen): "Greet Prisca and Aquila, who work with me in Christ Jesus, and who risked their necks for my life [in the silversmith riot], to whom not only I give thanks, but also all the churches of the Gentiles. Greet also the church in their house" (Romans 16:3-5).

AFTERWARD

Whether Prisca and Aquila were among those martyred during Nero's persecution of Christians in AD 64 remains uncertain, though seventh-century itineraries of pilgrimages to Rome mention their burial place in the registry of Roman martyrs' graves.

What is known for certain is the esteem in which Prisca was held by the early church. Luminaries such as Tertullian, Father of Latin theology, and John Chrysostom, a church doctor, give high praise to her work.

Prisca's name—and sometimes Aquila's too—regularly appears on biblical scholars' lists as a possible author of the Letter to the Hebrews. (The theme of her instruction of Apollos, "Jesus is the Messiah foretold in Scripture," is identical to the main theme of Hebrews.)

A testament to her evangelistic labors is the Church of St. Prisca, on the Aventine Hill in Rome. An ancient tradition says it is built over her house of apostolic times. House churches throughout the empire provided the foundation for early Christianity.

Around the time of the destruction of the temple in Jerusalem during a major Jewish uprising against Roman occupation in AD 70, the Christian sect was well on its way to breaking completely with Judaism.

In the following decades ecclesiastical machinery was developed to administer an expanding church. By the middle of the second century a manual for church officers had been compiled: the *Didache,* or "Teaching of the Twelve Apostles."

Cultural practices of the Greco-Roman world began to creep in, signified by the fact that women no longer were seated with men but formed a segregated part of the congregation. Nevertheless, Christians everywhere felt a sense of belonging to a universal institution.

LORD JESUS CHRIST,

I WONDER WHAT IT WAS LIKE,
WHEN PRISCA HEARD YOUR GOOD NEWS,
WHEN CHRISTIANITY WAS NEW.
IT FIRED WITHIN HER
THE NEED TO SHARE IT.

HELP ME TO HEAR THE GOSPELS
AS IF FOR THE FIRST TIME.
LET THE NEWNESS
REFRESH MY SOUL.
AMEN.

1 : PRISCA THE EVANGELIST

THE SECOND CENTURY

PERPETUA OF CARTHAGE

BACKGROUND

With the death of John the apostle about AD 100, the apostolic age drew to an end. After that, it became more important than ever to preserve in writing memories of Jesus' life and teachings as well as apostolic traditions.

Thus, in the second century the process was begun to determine which of the Gospels and other Christian literature circulating in that period were authentic and divinely inspired. By the end of the century there was general agreement regarding most of the books accepted as part of the New Testament, though the official list did not appear until the fourth century.

Other Christian literature important to this era included that of the apologists: writers who defined and defended the teachings of Christianity in order to counter the verbal and written attacks of pagan intellectuals. One prominent apologist, Irenaeus, became bishop in Lyons (France), replacing the bishop who was martyred in the persecution there in 177. Persecutions so far were sporadic and on a local basis, depending mostly on the whims of the local ruler.

Near the end of the second century a belief in the imminent Second Coming of Christ—a belief quite strong during the apostolic age—showed a resurgence, particularly among the faithful in North Africa. That prospect gave the faithful unusual courage.

In the summer of 180 seven men and five women of humble background were brought for trial to the capital city of Carthage from their own township of Scillium. The twelve were found guilty of being Christian and sentenced to beheading. The case of the Scillitan martyrs is history's first mention of the existence of Christianity in North Africa. How it became established is unclear, though one theory suggests that persons fleeing Nero's persecution in Rome may have brought the faith to the region. (Interestingly, Septimius Severus, who became emperor in 193, was of North African origin himself, as was Victor, bishop of Rome in the last decade of the second century.)

CARTHAGE, 180

In the same year in Thuburbo, a suburb of Carthage, a distinguished provincial family celebrates the birth of a girl they name Perpetua. The future looks rosy, for Roman Africa is just entering a period of considerable prosperity, as through the port of Carthage flow the agricultural riches of the provinces along with slaves for the empire.

Growing up in the comfortable and cultured environs of Carthage, Perpetua marries and has a baby of her own. As a young adult, she decides to become a Christian. (One of her brothers appears to have done so too. The rest of the family remains pagan, that is, abiding by the state religion with its nominal belief in patron gods and goddesses.)

Before being initiated into the Christian faith, the aspiring candidate—or catechumen, as one is called—must go through a process of instruction in the faith in addition to following a life of moral rectitude. This testing period lasts an average of two to three years, and therefore is not a decision taken lightly, with the obvious result that members remain on the whole a very dedicated people.

For every Christian, the possibility exists of being persecuted by the state for belonging to a sometimes suspect organization. Sporadic persecutions may occur in any province of the empire, perhaps at the whim of the local governor, or due to an outbreak of mob hostility provoked by calamities such as earthquake or epidemic. In an age abounding with superstition, people need a scapegoat, and Christians, so markedly different from the rest of the population, serve that purpose.

In the year 202 the empire experiences threats to national security on its frontiers along with insurrections in various places. Loyalty to the state consequently becomes a paramount issue. Since Christians preach nonviolence to the extent of resisting service in the army, Emperor Septimius Severus decides to issue an edict, to be implemented at the discretion of local authorities, requiring that all citizens prove their loyalty by making sacrifice to the gods of the empire. This, in effect, amounts to a renunciation of Christianity, with its insistence on belief in only one God.

To clamp down on any further spread of the faith, the edict outlaws efforts to make conversions. In other words, there are to be no more catechumens. (Incidentally, conversions to Judaism are also forbidden.) The resulting persecution is at its worst in Egypt and North Africa, probably because of the extraordinary fervor of these Christians. (Egypt was always considered a separate region from the North African provinces.)

The arrest of catechumens begins, and Perpetua is among them. She is part of a small group—three men and another woman (Felicitas, a slave in her household)—that is first placed under house arrest. While guarded in a private house for a brief period, the five catechumens manage to be baptized, and their lay instructor, Saturus, voluntarily joins them in confinement. The group is soon moved to the common prison in Carthage.

Once there, Perpetua keeps a diary that testifies vividly to the sufferings of a young woman from noble background who suddenly finds herself imprisoned even before a hearing on the case has occurred. "I was terrified," she writes, "as I had never before been in such a dark hole. What a difficult time it was!" She tells of the crowded conditions and the stifling heat. But most of all, she is "tortured with worry"[1] because of her infant son.

Perpetua gave the baby over to the care of her mother and a brother when they came to visit her. Later though, she gets permission to keep the baby with her. Without her son she found the place a "dungeon." But with the baby once more in her arms it becomes a "palace."

Though Perpetua never doubts that she has made the right decision in refusing to renounce her faith, still she must suffer for the anguish that choice causes her family—particularly her father who, as he reminds her, "favored you above all your brothers." He comes to the prison to plead with her for the sake of her son and for the sake of the family honor. Sadly, she refuses. "Think of your brothers, think of your mother and your aunt, think of your child," he implores. "Give up your pride! You will destroy all of us!"[2]

"This was the way my father spoke out of love for me," Perpetua reflects as she goes on to describe her efforts to comfort him, assuring him that what happens in the prisoner's dock will all happen as God wills. "And he left me in great sorrow."[3] (Perpetua never mentions her husband in the diary, though tradition tells us that she is "respectably married." Aside from that, there can only be speculation.)

While waiting for a hearing and uncertain when it will be, Perpetua reluctantly relinquishes the baby to her father during one of his visits. Then, during breakfast one morning, the prisoners are suddenly hurried off to the forum. In the crowd that quickly gathers, Perpetua sees her father with the baby. He begs his daughter to sacrifice to the gods. To offer incense, a simple statement of loyalty to the empire, seems little enough if it will save her life.

Hilarianus, the official hearing the case, adds his bit: "Have pity on your father's grey head; have pity on your infant son. Offer the sacrifice for the welfare of the emperors."

Perpetua, though, cannot deny her faith in the one true God. "I will not," she says adamantly.

"Are you a Christian?" Hilarianus asks. And she replies, "Yes, I am."

When her father continues pleading with her, Hilarianus orders him to be thrown to the ground and beaten. For Perpetua it is "just as if I myself had been beaten."

None of the others will recant either. They are sentenced to fight wild beasts in the amphitheater, and then returned to prison to await the scheduled date.

Perpetua hopes that she will be allowed to have the baby with her until the sentence is carried out, but her father refuses. But because the baby no longer needs to be nursed at the breast, she confides to her diary, "I was relieved of any anxiety for my child."[4]

She receives consoling visions, which help her to remain at peace. Saturus, the catechumens' instructor who chose to join them in prison, also keeps a diary. In it he writes of a vision in which he sees their death, and then "when we were free of this world, we first saw an intense light."[5]

At this point, the writings of Perpetua and Saturus end. Their precious document is entrusted to someone for safekeeping. The rest of the story comes to us from an eyewitness, sometimes referred to as the redactor.

As the account continues, we learn that Secundulus, one of their number, has died in prison, perhaps from harsh treatment. Others, meanwhile, find comfort in hearing about the conversion of the adjutant in charge of the jail. Their greatest concern relates to Felicitas's, the slave's, condition. She fears that she might not be able to die in the arena with the others because of her pregnancy. (Her execution will simply be postponed.) As the time for her delivery draws near, the group prays that it will be soon. Labor pains ensue, and she gives birth two days before the date of execution. Another Christian woman comes forward, taking the baby to raise as her own.

The last meal for the condemned customarily takes place in a room open to the public. The room is filled with spectators as the five companions-in-death turn the occasion into an agape, or love-feast, an early Christian tradition consisting of prayer, a supper and the singing of psalms and hymns. (The shared meal of the agape symbolized the love Christians felt for each other. In apostolic times it had customarily been held in connection with the eucharistic service.) Some of the onlookers ridicule them, but others express only admiration for the dignity with which the group conducts itself that evening.

On the morning of March 7, 203, the prisoners are marched from the prison to the amphitheater, with a capacity of about thirty thousand, where they will form part of the public entertainment during festivities marking the emperor's birthday. The group goes joyfully, and Perpetua is described as having a "shining countenance and calm step...putting down everyone's stare by her own intense gaze."[6]

The men are forced to put on the robes worn by priests of Saturn, god of harvests. When the women are given the dress for priestesses of Ceres, a goddess associated with fertility rites, Perpetua resists, arguing with the tribune. He agrees that the women have been told they will not have to wear it.

At the insistence of the spectators, the prisoners are scourged before being mauled by wild animals let loose in the arena. The first two, Saturninus and Revocatus, are attacked by a bear. Perpetua and Felicitas go next, matched against a mad heifer. Stripped naked and put into nets, they are brought into the arena. For a change, the crowd expresses horror at seeing that one of the young women is "fresh from childbirth with the milk still dripping from her breasts."[7] This prompts officials to have the women dressed in tunics.

When Perpetua is tossed into the air by the mad heifer, her tunic rips along the side. More concerned about modesty than her pain, she pulls at the tunic to cover her exposed thighs, then rearranges her disheveled hair. She sees Felicitas in a heap on the ground and hurries over to give her a hand, lifting her up. The two stand side by side, a noble matron and her personal slave, facing death as sisters.

For the moment, the crowd's appetite for violence appears satisfied, and the women are allowed to retreat. Passing near several catechumens, including her brother (who has escaped arrest), Perpetua says, "You must all *stand fast in the faith* and love one another, and do not be weakened by what we have gone through."[8]

Saturus enters the arena last. When the gladiator begins tying the prisoner to a wild boar, he himself is gored by the animal.

Saturus is next matched against a bear that refuses to come out of its cage. Finally a leopard is let loose, and with one savage bite drenches Saturus in blood.

Still, the entire group has thus far survived the attacks, which means they must be put to death by the sword. The mob clamors for the prisoners to be brought into the open where they can witness the bloody spectacle.

Assembling in full view, the five give each other the ritual kiss of peace before each is executed by the sword. Perpetua's turn comes last. The gladiator assigned to dispatch her nervously takes poor aim. His hand slips and the sword strikes bone. Perpetua emits a brief scream, but "then she took the trembling hand of the young gladiator and guided it to her throat."[9]

AFTERWARD

The treasury of early Christian writings was enhanced by a genre of literature known as the "Acts of the Martyrs." Some of the stories came from official trial records, others from descriptions by eyewitnesses. Still others are obvious embellishments intended to inspire the listener.

The account titled "The Martyrdom of Saints Perpetua and Felicitas" is especially valued as an authentic firsthand narration. Perpetua's diary comprises the greater part, then the account by Saturus. Both introduction and conclusion were composed by an observer at the scene (commonly thought to be the Carthaginian theologian Tertullian, though it has been suggested that the redactor may have been one of the deacons who visited the group in prison to give moral support).

During the succeeding hundred years of the empire's periodic and severe persecutions of Christians, the story of Perpetua, one of the early church's most revered martyrs, would give sustenance to the faithful, drawing them closer together. In recognition of the young woman's sacrifice, her diary was often read during worship services (as were other selections from the "Acts").

For a number of years, an annual festival honoring her took place at the great basilica in Carthage, where her relics were preserved. The shrine no longer exists and the relics have since been lost, but Perpetua's memory is kept universally alive by the inclusion of her name in the First Eucharistic Prayer. To Tertullian is owed the observation that "the blood of martyrs is the seed of the church." Proof of that was seen in the continued growth of Christianity despite all attempts to eliminate the followers of Christ.

O DIVINE PRESENCE,

YOU WERE WITH PERPETUA,
WEREN'T YOU?
THROUGH HER DAYS OF IMPRISONMENT
AND THAT AWFUL DAY IN THE ARENA,
WHEN SHE VALIANTLY KEPT THE FAITH.

IN THE TRIALS OF LIFE
THAT SEND ME TO MY KNEES,
I DISCOVER ANEW
YOU ARE WITH ME, TOO.
AMEN.

THE THIRD CENTURY

Apollonia of Alexandria

Background

With the end of Severus's persecution (he died in 211), Christians in the African part of the empire found themselves blessed with a "long peace," as church history terms it. Succeeding emperors were busy dealing with other matters, such as Rome's loss of power to control its frontiers. The church, left undisturbed, used the ensuing four decades to expand its own frontiers: making conversions, defining doctrines and developing ministries in more organized fashion. Bishops, who were chosen by the members of each Christian community, served as a unifying force; ecclesiastical sees kept in contact with each other by letters or at meetings. One synod in Carthage in 220, for example, saw seventy-one bishops from the provinces of North Africa in attendance.

The long peace notwithstanding, Christians could never become too complacent, for the superstitious pagan population surrounding them was in the habit of blaming Christians whenever things went wrong. And conditions were worsening everywhere—politically, economically and socially. Trouble struck first in Alexandria, signaling that the Christians' era of peace was over.

ALEXANDRIA, 249

In this city on Egypt's Mediterranean seacoast, a mob is incited to torture and put to death a number of men and women simply because of their identity as Christians.

In a letter to the bishop of Antioch, Dionysius, the bishop of Alexandria, describes the terrible ordeals suffered by members of his congregation. Among the tragedies he recounts: "Next they seized the wonderful old lady Apollonia, battered her till they knocked out all her teeth, built a pyre in front of the city, and threatened to burn her alive unless she repeated after them their heathen incantations. She asked for a breathing-space, and when they released her, jumped without hesitation into the fire and was burned to ashes."[1]

As the mob's intentions were clear and since she had no intention of renouncing her faith, Apollonia chose to embrace death voluntarily rather than be dragged into the fire. The early church esteemed Apollonia both for the courageous way she chose death rather than renounce her faith and for the many years she served the Christian community in Alexandria as a deaconess. So well-known did her record become, a church built in Rome was dedicated in her honor.

Yet, despite acclaim by contemporaries, little of a personal nature regarding Apollonia's life was preserved. Still, a likely picture can be sketched, based on historical information about third-century Alexandria, its Christian community and, in particular, the role of deaconesses. Add to that the wealth of meaning implied in the bishop's description: "wonderful old lady."

At the time of her death, Apollonia was somewhere between seventy and eighty years old. Her birth would have occurred in the latter part of the second century, quite possibly between 170 and 180—roughly the time Perpetua of Carthage was born. Though Apollonia's life spanned parts of two centuries, most of it was lived in the third, a period when the church entered into significant growth both in terms of organization and as a spiritual force. To look at Apollonia's probable career in Christian ministry is to see the unfolding of ecclesiastical development.

Apollonia survived Emperor Severus's persecution, which took many lives in Egypt as well as in North Africa. The same year the persecution ended, 203, marked a milestone for Alexandria's Catechetical School; it fell heir to a director named Origen. (Dionysius headed it before becoming bishop.) Under Origen's tutelage, the school was destined to become renowned in intellectual circles. It drew great minds to the church, including philosophers disillusioned by pagan thinking. This helped to put the faith on a sound theological basis.

Alexandria was the logical place for this to happen. The city had long enjoyed a reputation for learning. It possessed one of the great libraries of the ancient world, with an unrivaled four hundred thousand volumes.

The Catechetical School had begun, as the name indicates, for catechumens: men and women receiving instruction for baptism. Even as the school expanded to cover theological and philosophical courses, both sexes continued to be enrolled as students. Both also performed secretarial duties as amanuenses, trained to take dictation and copy manuscripts by hand. Whether Apollonia ever served in this capacity is not known although as a deaconess responsible for instructing catechumens she would have been well acquainted with the workings of the school.

By her time the Christian community in Alexandria was long established. According to Western historians, the exact date of the faith's founding is shrouded in mystery, though the Christian community definitely existed by the second century. Eastern historians, especially the Egyptian Christian ones, trace the beginnings to the arrival of Mark the Evangelist, whom their tradition says founded the first Christian community in Alexandria—always a point of great pride to its faithful. In Mark's day the city's population numbered about one million, a fourth of them Jewish—providing fertile ground for initial conversions. (Tradition tells us that Mark met martyrdom in Alexandria.)

For a certainty, the faith had taken firm hold in both Upper and Lower Egypt by the end of the second century, when young people like Apollonia were committing themselves to a lifetime of discipleship to gospel ideals. In the midst of an essentially pagan society, they had to wrestle with the difficulties of maintaining high moral standards.

One eminent churchman, Clement of Alexandria, cautioned the young woman tempted to adopt some of the pagan practices in fashion: "What shall we say of love of ornament, dyed materials, the vanity of colours, the luxury of jewels, goldwork, hair waved or curled, eyes mascaraed, eyebrows plucked, rouge, ceruse [a cosmetic containing white lead], dyed hair and all these deceitful artifices?"[2]

Not all temptations proved quite so venial, however. There was, for instance, the social institution of public baths, where mixed nude bathing led to promiscuous behavior by some. Another popular leisure activity, attending the theater, posed problems, too, for performances frequently contained obscene material. In such an atmosphere, the Christian had to continually exert vigilance.

Candidates for acceptance into the faith must prove themselves capable of leading a moral life in addition to going through several years of instruction. In the formation of female candidates, the deaconess played a primary role.

Though the ministry dates back to apostolic times, the deaconess really came into her own during the great expansion of the church during the third century. Another ministry, the order of widows, also originated in the primitive church, and during Apollonia's younger years this order still held preeminence. The widows' duties were to pray and to visit the sick. For admission, a woman must be sixty years or older. But great age sometimes meant that a widow was not always able to meet the demands involved in attending to the sick.

As conversions increased, service to the community became more and more the prerogative of the deaconess, whose ministry went beyond that of the widows to encompass a variety of pastoral, liturgical and educational duties. The deaconess at this time played a more vital part in the church in the East than in the West, which seemed always reluctant to accept the deaconess as a recognized institution. Alexandria, though a crossroads of the two regions, tended culturally toward the East.

For the female half of church membership, a woman acting as minister was an absolute necessity in a number of situations in order to avoid any hint of scandal. The sacrament of baptism had evolved from a simple water ritual into an elaborate ceremony. Early in the third century, Christians began building houses specifically designed for worship. The baptistery, with its pool or cistern, was a major feature. The oldest surviving example of this architecture is in Dura-Europos, Syria. Adult candidates disrobed before stepping into the pool used for the rite. What's more, the anointing of the whole body made it a matter of propriety for a woman to preside during that part of the rite.

Clement of Alexandria, an early contemporary of Apollonia (he died c. 215), pictures precisely what her role would have been:

First of all, when women descend into the water for baptism, it is necessary that those who thus descend should be anointed with the oil of unction by the Deaconess.... The minister normally only anoints the head where women are concerned; it is the customary role of the Deaconess to anoint the body.

...When she who is baptized comes out of the water, the Deaconess shall receive her, instruct her, and look after her, to the end that the unbreakable seal of baptism may be impressed on her with purity and holiness.[3]

The deaconess looked after her charges not just during the baptismal rite but throughout the entire period of candidacy. While the eucharistic liturgy took place on Sunday, catechumens might have met daily with their deaconess for prayer and Scripture instruction, with emphasis on the Christian way of life. The newly baptized, or neophytes, afterward remained for a time the responsibility of the deaconess.

She proved her worth in other respects, too, as Clement further noted: "Where Christian women live in heathen households it is necessary that it should be the Deaconess who goes there and visits women who are sick."[4] Clearly, she inherited the pastoral duty of the order of widows. At the eucharistic liturgy the deaconess functioned as doorkeeper, standing at the entrance to the women's section and making sure that decorum was maintained.

All Christians, not only special ministers such as the deaconess, had an enviable reputation among the surrounding pagan society on account of the extraordinary spirit of love they demonstrated in caring for the poor and the sick, whether of their own faith or not. During epidemics, when pagan households in dread of contagion put their ailing and dying members into the street, the victims were routinely rescued by Christians.

Yet despite such heroic witness, the minority inevitably came in for mistreatment themselves whenever people's fears were exploited. As conditions in the empire worsened, the government saw a need once more to underscore a mood of patriotism, traditionally solidified behind the state religion. A year before the Emperor Decius issued an edict requiring citizens to prove loyalty by sacrifice to state gods, a pagan priest in Alexandria stirred up the mob that brought about Apollonia's martyrdom as well as that of many others. That "wonderful old lady"—one of the countless to whom the church owes its survival—would receive universal recognition for the final act of her long lifetime of service, as we have seen, because one bishop happened to write a letter to another bishop.

AFTERWARD

The year following Apollonia's death the short but severe Decian persecution was the first systematic effort of the imperial administration to wipe out the church. After that, as before, periods of relative peace for Christians alternated with times of trouble. By far the worst empire-wide persecution was launched in 303 during Diocletian's reign as emperor. Egypt bore the brunt with a reported 144,000 Christians put to the sword. (Scholars today are inclined to dispute such a large figure.) In reporting on martyrdoms, Eusebius, a church historian in that era, observes that "there were occasions when on a single day a hundred men as well as women and little children were killed, condemned to a succession of ever-changing punishments."[5] He describes some of the horrors endured by them. Whatever the precise number, Eusebius makes clear the immensity of the suffering. Despite persecution, by early in the fourth century, Christians constituted the majority of the population in Egypt. The faith had been firmly rooted by servants of the church such as Apollonia.

When the new emperor, Constantine, granted freedom of worship in 313, abruptly changing the fortunes of the faith, asceticism and consequent celibacy began to take the place of martyrdom as the "highest call" to discipleship.

Once the religion was state-approved, conversions came in greater numbers than ever before, making impossible the lengthy, individualized process of instruction. The shift to baptizing the very young rather than waiting for adulthood further lessened the need for the deaconess. Ministry was on its way to being associated with male priesthood.

Monasticism increasingly seemed almost the sole outlet for the woman eager to dedicate herself to the service of God, although the female diaconate continued to function as part of the ecclesiastical structure for some time yet in the eastern half of the church.

HOLY SPIRIT,

IT IS AMAZING WHAT FEATS OF COURAGE
A SPIRIT-FILLED PERSON CAN DO.
YET IT IS NOT THE LAST ACT
OF APOLLONIA'S LIFE THAT FILLS ME WITH AWE,
BUT HER YEARS AND YEARS OF MINISTRY.

HELP ME TO REMAIN STEADFAST, TOO,
SO THAT AT THE END OF MY DAYS,
THEY WILL SAY OF ME,
"SHE WAS A WONDERFUL OLD LADY."
AMEN.

THE FOURTH CENTURY

MACRINA OF CAPPADOCIA

BACKGROUND

Won over to the faith, Emperor Constantine took an active role, convening the first ecumenical council in the history of the young church. Some three hundred bishops from around the empire accepted the invitation, though the aging bishop of Rome declined, sending two representatives in his stead. Meeting in Nicaea (northwest Asia Minor) in 325, the council's primary intention was to do something about a controversial priest in Alexandria named Arius, who was preaching that Christ was only human and not the Son of God. Constantine banished the priest, and the council formulated the Nicene Creed. The heretical doctrine itself was not as easily disposed of as Arius. In fact, when Constantine finally accepted baptism on his deathbed in 337, the rite was performed by an Arian bishop.

A year or two after the council, Constantine sent his mother, Helena, then in her late seventies, on a mission to the Holy Land to verify the sites made sacred by Jesus' life. As a result of her work, a spiritual force was unleashed and pilgrimage to the holy places became the goal of devout Christians.

In 330 Constantine moved the capital of the empire from Rome to Constantinople, building a city named, of course, in his honor over the site of ancient Byzantium. This move to a more geographically defensible position shifted the empire's base of influence eastward. Among the centers of trade in the East was the city of Caesarea in Cappadocia (present-day Turkey). And among the city's distinguished families was that of Basil the Elder.

CAESAREA, C. 340

"[M]any men wanted to marry her on account of the reputation of her beauty,"[1] so wrote Gregory of Nyssa in "The Life of St. Macrina." He surely knew, for Gregory's subject was his sister. (Elsewhere he praised her intellect and sanctity.)

At this time Macrina is about twelve or thirteen, the customary age when parents arranged marriage for a daughter. Although she has no desire for marriage, Macrina accedes to her father's wishes. His choice for her is a young man of great promise, one already noted as an orator and a defender of the "wronged" in lawsuits. But before the wedding ceremony can take place, the man dies unexpectedly.

Macrina's father, Basil the Elder, would have chosen another fiancé for her. But this time she resolves to follow her own design, made before the ill-fated betrothal: to live as a consecrated virgin while remaining at home as companion to her mother. Although Basil is a skilled lawyer, he finds his daughter's counterargument persuasive: that she cannot marry another, for her "husband" is merely absent, away on a journey to God, and she must "keep faith with an absent husband."[2] Her novel reasoning gets support from her mother, Emmelia, who before Macrina's birth learned in a vision that her firstborn would be a special child. Basil must share that view, for Macrina wins her case.

Shortly after, Basil dies, leaving Emmelia with ten children. Macrina, as the oldest, immediately takes over the care of the youngest, infant Peter, in addition to sustaining her mother in her grief. Fortunately they have no financial worries, for the family owns landed estates in three provinces. Despite her age, Macrina proves adept in the management of business affairs. And even though the household is staffed with servants, she doesn't neglect domestic chores either. She shows remarkable skill in spinning wool and "making bread for her mother with her own hands,"[3] as Gregory admiringly relates. Above all, Macrina passes on to her five brothers and four sisters the principles of a good moral life, drawing on the solid grounding in Scripture provided by her parents since her early childhood. Gregory remembers that she was "my teacher in all things."[4]

Once the children are grown, the family wealth is apportioned among them. (Naucratius, the brother dearest to Macrina, has in the interim died in an accident while helping the poor.) Arrangements are made for the four sisters—presumably marriage. Gregory refers to them in only the briefest way. Finally Macrina's longed-for dream is about to come true.

In the preceding years, she has gradually led her mother along the path to a contemplative lifestyle. Now, around the year 355, she persuades Emmelia to establish an ascetic community of women on one of the family estates: at Annisa, a pastoral setting on the Iris River in Pontus, the province north of Caesarea.

According to plan, they take the household maids, who will live with them as sisters in this new arrangement, sharing the same food, accommodations and manual labor. They will share, too, as equals in the spiritual life, to be fostered by asceticism and prayer. There are, in fact, two branches of the community slated: one for women and another for men, with Macrina's youngest brother Peter included among the latter.

The history of a consecrated life for women began with the New Testament "order of widows": older women committed to lives of chastity, prayer and good works within their Christian congregation. It wasn't long before younger women were able to become deaconesses.

Many chose to consecrate themselves to virginity. Various ways of living out that radical commitment developed. Some remained "in the world" but wore black or gray to set them apart from other unmarried women. Consecration might consist of a church ceremony in which the bishop bestowed a blessed veil, or it may be made publicly visible when the hair—a woman's "glory"—was shorn as an act of renunciation. Whether living at home or with a small group of other consecrated virgins, the women would fast, pray and labor—much like contemplative nuns today.

History tells us that Antony of Egypt, venerated as the "Father of Monasticism," left his younger sister in the care of a community of ascetic virgins ("convent" is the term used by Antony's biographer Athanasius) before taking up the life himself in the desert about 270. (There were at the time no similar institutions for men.)

Around the year 320 another Egyptian, Pachomius, expanded on Antony's concept but emphasized the community aspect of monasticism. His sister Mary was eager to grow in the spiritual life too, and soon the desert flourished with communities of nuns as well as monks. (These were the Desert Fathers and Mothers who graced that period of church history.) Mary had already established her first convent near Tabennisi on the banks of the Nile when Macrina felt inspired to initiate a similar project. Because her family then lived in Caesarea, a major city of the empire, they undoubtedly heard of events transpiring in the "Holy Land," as people called Egypt in honor of the thousands of devout men and women intent on recapturing the gospel ideal of lives spent in love and service to each other.

Following the Peace of Constantine and the end of persecution, Christianity found itself becoming the state religion. As a result, the church tended toward increasing involvement in politics and other secular matters. Monasticism originated as a lay movement in opposition to this growing worldliness.

Macrina's style of monastic life at Annisa differs from the Egyptian model in several respects. The most obvious is the physical environment: woods and valleys rather than desert sands. But more importantly, in her version the monastic community reaches out to the broader community around it, engaging in works of mercy. For example, Macrina goes out and literally picks up women lying on the road in a state of starvation. (Unless a woman was independently wealthy or provided for by a father, brother or husband, her well-being remained at risk.) After being nursed back to health, those rescued seem glad to stay on as members of Annisa. And whatever their age, they call Macrina "mother."

Charitable works are another feature of her monastery. She establishes a hospital for the poor in connection with Annisa. When a terrible famine strikes this part of the world, no one who comes for help is turned away due to brother Peter's foresight in storing up provisions. "[T]he large numbers going to and fro," writes Gregory, "makes the hermitage seem like a city."[5]

While Peter has from the start worked alongside his sister and mother, Gregory has married and Basil has established a school of rhetoric in Caesarea. Basil, because of Macrina's inspiration and persuasion, as he would later recount, decides to join her monastic endeavor. Before doing so, however, he makes a tour of communities in Egypt, Syria, Palestine and Mesopotamia, then returns to govern the men's quarters at Annisa as abbot. He stays only a few years, however, before going back to the city to aid the bishop in fighting the heresy of Arianism.

In that sojourn as a monk, Basil—"the Great" is the title his later prominence would confer on him—devises a rule of life for monks still used by the Eastern Orthodox Church. When he becomes bishop of Caesarea in 370, Basil continues to follow his sister's example, founding charitable institutions, including a hospital for the poor similar to the one at Annisa.

Gregory, too, succumbs to Macrina's appeals, gives up the secular life and is ordained a priest. (His wife may have already died. In any case, celibacy is not yet mandatory.) Like Basil, he engages in fighting Arianism, a doctrine denying the divinity of Christ, and enjoys the distinction of being one of the leading theologians in the East.

After her mother's death, about 370, Macrina gives all her wealth to the poor. The center at Annisa must, therefore, support itself solely by its own labor, earning income through handwork such as spinning (one of Macrina's domestic achievements as a girl) and sometimes copying manuscripts.

The convent continues to grow because of the attraction it holds: giving women an opportunity to use their gifts. Society otherwise allows them little in the way of self-development. Neither does the church utilize their talents in ministry as in pre-Constantine times. Current thinking regarding women's capabilities in comparison to that of men's is manifest from the very first page of Gregory's "Life" of his sister: "We spoke of a woman, if one may refer to her as that, for I do not know if it is right to use that natural designation for one who went beyond the nature of a woman."[6]

Gregory's most lavish praise for his beloved sister is prompted by a visit to her on his return from an important church gathering in Constantinople. He has not seen Macrina for some years because of difficulties arising from his courageous defense of the faith; he suffered exile when pro-Arian rulers sat on the throne.

Their brother Basil died only a few months before, and now Gregory is grieved to find his sister seriously ill. He also becomes fully cognizant of her "angelic existence" at Annisa. Despite a feverish state, she continues to live as always: sleeping on a board on the ground with another board as her pillow.

They speak of Basil's death and, in the course of an extended discussion, Macrina expresses lofty thoughts on death and the resurrection of the soul which will serve as the basis for Gregory's great work, *On the Soul and the Resurrection*. (He is careful to give her credit.)

After a while, Macrina tells her brother that surely he must be weary from his long journey and advises him to get some rest.

When later their conversation is resumed, they speak of times past and the legacy of faith they inherited, not just from their parents. Gregory recalls that, "Our father's parents had been deprived of their possessions because of the confession of Christ; our mother's grandfather was killed by the anger of the emperor and all his property handed over to other masters. Nevertheless, their life was so exalted on account of their faith that no one had a greater reputation among the men of that time."[7]

On a different note, Gregory begins to complain of his problems with the pro-Arian Emperor Valens and of all the disputes within the church he is constantly called on to settle due to his prominence. She scolds him, telling Gregory that his fame is not due to anything on his part but "the prayers of your parents," she says, "are lifting you to the heights, since you have little or nothing within yourself by which to achieve this."[8] (In times past, she had likewise straightened out their brother Basil who, as a young man, was "puffed up" with pride.) Evidently, Gregory accepts her words with humility, since he records them.

In his sister's last hours, Gregory continues to be inspired by her example: "It was as if an angel had by some providence taken on human form."[9]

Later, making funeral preparations, Gregory asks for some burial attire other than her simple gown and worn sandals. Learning that this is all she has, so austerely did she live, he covers her body with his episcopal cloak. Finally, Gregory witnesses the affection in which Macrina is held as shown by the tremendous grief of both the Annisa community and the crowds of mourners who come from all parts of the province.

AFTERWARD

In a family remarkable for the number of saints it produced— Macrina's mother, father, grandmother (Macrina the Elder), three brothers—Macrina is the one dubbed holy and great. For the Eastern Church she provided the model for a women's religious community. The "spiritual kingdom" of the convent promised intellectual as well as spiritual growth and, incidentally, escape from the arranged and often unwelcome marriage. Asceticism was a small price to pay for such gains.

Macrina pioneered further in developing the concept of social welfare in connection with monasticism, an idea picked up by the church in the West and one of inestimable value for the future.

In a golden age of writings by church fathers, supporters behind the scenes often were sisters, mothers or female friends. Take, for example, Jerome, noted for translating the Bible into Latin. Late in the fourth century, he and some from his circle of noble Roman ladies went to Bethlehem, where he wrote while they served as helpmates and also founded monastic houses.

Back in the Roman monastic circle, women did scholarly Scripture studies, though none of the writings were apparently preserved. Macrina's voice, of course, is heard through the work of her famous brothers. Proof of what women were capable of may be seen in Egeria's *Diary of a Pilgrimage*. Of independent means, highly literate and perhaps a nun, she journeyed widely through Egypt, Syria and Palestine to as far as Mesopotamia (today's Iraq), leaving an account of her travels to churches, shrines and monasteries. The manuscript, which was discovered in a library in Italy in 1884, provides valuable data on liturgical practices in the East at the turn of the century (c. 400).

BLESSED LORD,

CALM IN RESOLVE
EVEN IN HER YOUTH,
MACRINA LED HER FAMILY
INTO LIVES OF SAINTLINESS,
OF SERVICE TO THOSE IN NEED.

IN MY OWN FAMILY LIFE,
WHAT MAY I DO?
SHOW ME THE WAY, LORD,
TO MAKE MY FAMILY HOLY, TOO.
AMEN.

THE FIFTH CENTURY

PULCHERIA OF CONSTANTINOPLE

BACKGROUND

Like his predecessors, Theodosius the Great was a Roman emperor who involved himself in church business—but not just to engage in weighty matters such as stamping out Arianism and other heresies. Theodosius also got down to the finer points of ecclesiastical administration. In 390, for example, he issued a decree that forbade women to come to church if, "contrary to human and divine law," they were so bold as to cut their hair. There were even sanctions against the bishop who allowed a shorn woman to attend church. To Theodosius's credit, he was willing to apply standards of obedience to himself as well. Once when ordered to do public penance by a bishop for an act judged sinful, he complied.

Imperial standards were lowered when his son Arcadius succeeded him to the throne at Constantinople in 395. During
Arcadius's reign the revered John Chrysostom became patriarch
(archbishop) of Constantinople, a leading position in the church
at large. After incurring the enmity of the emperor's wife Eudoxia,
John was stripped of his episcopacy. The weak-willed Arcadius sat
back while Eudoxia managed the ugly business, allying herself
with the patriarch of Alexandria, who had earlier had a run-in
with the fearlessly upright John Chrysostom. Byzantine politics,
secular or ecclesiastical, were messy.

CONSTANTINOPLE, JULY 4, 414

Arcadius's fifteen-year-old daughter Pulcheria ascends the throne
to act as regent and guardian for her younger brother, Theodosius
II. Since their father's death in 408, the Roman Empire has been
without its traditional emperor. Although a minister of state has
governed well during the interim (their mother's death predated
the father's), the people long for royalty to lead. And since
Pulcheria shows such a grasp of affairs, she is chosen to take the
reigns of government until her brother, two years younger,
acquires the necessary maturity.

Pulcheria's grandfather, Theodosius the Great, had earlier
divided the Roman Empire into East and West; each half was governed by one of his sons. When invasion by Germanic tribes
seemed imminent, the capital in the West was moved in 404, far-
ther north to Ravenna, a more defensible location. Now only the
bishop of Rome remains to keep order in that beleaguered city.
Constantinople, in a far more secure position, has grown to be
the center of power and wealth for the empire.

Pulcheria has no easy job, ruling from a city known for its
political plots and counterplots, corruption and high passions. In
one of her first public acts, performed in the Great Church of
Constantinople, she vows to live within the precincts of the royal

court as a consecrated virgin. Her two younger sisters vow the same. Compared to the recent past, when their parents' lifestyle was described as "riotous," the new atmosphere makes the palace seem almost monastic.

Brother Theodosius and the three sisters fast twice a week, study and pray. The young women forsake cosmetics and extravagant dress. Pulcheria's piety extends further—to building churches, establishing shelters for the homeless, founding monastic communities and providing for their support from her personal fortune.

In a court ever hungry for scandal, Pulcheria takes great care to avoid even a hint of it. She does not speak with any man save in public places. By refusing to marry, she avoids others' ambitious schemes to create political alliances that may not be best for the empire—or for her brother's position. Though Theodosius bears the title of emperor (hers is the imperial Augusta), he lacks Pulcheria's shrewdness—or "manly spirit," as the historian Gibbon will later put it. Rather, he prefers such pursuits as hunting and painting, and depends on his sister to exercise power for the royal family. His education has also been entrusted to her, and she oversees this with typical thoroughness. Theodosius emerges well-educated, but his vacillating nature remains the same.

Reaching the age of twenty, he asks Pulcheria to find him a bride, stressing that beauty ranks before all else, even before royal background. None in the female population of Constantinople suits him. Instead he falls in love with Athenais, the beautiful and intelligent daughter of an Athenian philosopher. After she has been baptized a Christian and her pagan name changed to Eudokia, the wedding takes place.

For a time after that Pulcheria goes on administering state affairs while Eudokia is occupied with domestic matters, giving birth to a girl in 422. The following year her adoring husband grants Eudokia the title "Augusta," the same title previously given Pulcheria. Eudokia begins to resent the influence her sister-in-law has over Theodosius, and trouble is not long in coming. Sharing the same palace roof becomes impossible. And so Pulcheria decides to ease the situation by moving, along with her sisters, to one of their suburban palaces where the three continue to live ascetically while engaging in many philanthropic works.

Pulcheria, however, does not abandon her interest in state affairs, or ecclesiastical ones either. In the church of the East, debate over religious matters is practically a national pastime. Butcher, baker and just about everyone else—all consider themselves amateur theologians. Passions rise and quarrels erupt into fistfights.

One of the most emotionally charged subjects is the Blessed Virgin, a figure deeply revered by the majority. When in 428 a priest preaches the impossibility of a human becoming "Mother of God," he provokes a near-riot in the church where he speaks. Nevertheless, Nestorius, the Patriarch of Constantinople, takes up the idea, arguing that Mary should be called Christ-Bearer, not God-Bearer. (Theologians of the period accept church teaching that Jesus was both human and divine, but the relationship between the two natures has yet to be defined.)

Battle lines are quickly drawn, hardened the more by Nestorius's dogmatic position. Into the fray steps Eudokia, who lines up with the patriarch. Upholding the opposite, orthodox view, Pulcheria is joined by a leading light in the church, Cyril, patriarch of Alexandria. Both sides accuse the other of heresy, while Theodosius squirms uncomfortably in the middle. (The emperor's voice is expected to be the controlling one in church matters.)

He wavers between wife and sister. The winner is evident when Theodosius calls a general council of bishops to meet at

Ephesus in 431 and Cyril is chosen to preside. The council proclaims Mary the "Mother of God." Nestorius is forced to step down as patriarch and is banished to Egypt.

Seeing Pulcheria as engineering the defeat of Nestorius, his partisans initiate a campaign of slander against her (though she wins praise from Pope Leo the Great). Theodosius apparently pays no attention to the scurrilous rumors, for he and his sister proceed to work on projects of importance, such as the compilation into sixteen volumes of the Theodosian Code of Law, later a basis for much legislation in Western Europe.

Eudokia, meanwhile, is busy with a project of her own: arranging the marriage of her only daughter to the emperor of the West, thereby uniting the two royal families. But following this triumph, trouble appears to arise between her and Theodosius. Some speculate it is because of her inability to bear a son.

In early 438 Pulcheria, to make amends for her late mother's ill treatment of the holy John Chrysostom (whose criticism of the woman's morals had led to his exile and death), arranges to have his body returned and buried with honor in a Constantinople church. It is a highly popular move. We find no mention that Eudokia is present at the ceremony. Soon after, she leaves for a pilgrimage to the Holy Land, ostensibly in thanksgiving for her daughter's happy marriage.

Upon her return a year later, a very ambitious court eunuch named Chrysaphius conspires with the politically inexperienced Eudokia to turn Theodosius against his sister and eliminate Pulcheria's influence. (In the Byzantine court it was not unusual for a eunuch, perhaps originally employed as an attendant to the emperor, to advance to a position with significant powers, such as palace chamberlain.)

Part of the plot involves having Pulcheria ordained a deaconess, for that function will exclude her from any role in government. One of Pulcheria's allies in the hierarchy warns her, and she promptly retires to her palace in Hebdomon to avoid ordination. But this leaves the way open for Chrysaphius to gain full control over the well-intentioned but weak-willed Theodosius. (In the meantime, the unhappy Eudokia returns to Jerusalem in 443 to stay permanently. There she will devote the rest of her life to charitable and pious acts.)

Pulcheria's one source of power remains that of a holy woman, for so the people of Constantinople regard her. (In fact, a bishop has her image painted above the altar of the Great Church.)

Though adept at gaining power, Chrysaphius shows himself no match for Pulcheria in managing the empire's business, which suffers as a result. Another theological crisis will plague him. That trouble starts with his godfather Eutyches, the superior of a monastery who also enjoys a favored position at court, for he is among those under the protection of the eunuch.

Eutyches previously led the most violent opposition to Nestorianism. Gradually he comes to advocating the idea that Christ's humanity was absorbed in his divinity: a proposition labeled Monophysitism, or belief that Jesus had only one nature.

When Flavian, now patriarch of Constantinople, deposes Eutyches for his teaching, the latter appeals for help. Theodosius is prevailed upon to convene another general council of the church at Ephesus in 449. At a chaotic gathering, soldiers compel those in attendance to vote the way of Eutyches (and his sponsor, Chrysaphius)—causing it to be called "the Robber Council." Flavian is roughed up before he is deposed as patriarch and imprisoned, where he dies. Theodosius upholds the council's decision, and Pulcheria for the moment is helpless to do anything despite appeals from Pope Leo in Rome.

But Chrysaphius's days are numbered, for Theodosius decides that he has had his fill of a poorly managed empire. In the spring of 450 he recalls his sister to resume administration of the government. Just a few months later, when Theodosius's fall from a horse proves fatal, Pulcheria becomes sole ruler of the empire—the first woman ever to do so.

Understanding the prudence of governing with a husband at her side in the present circumstances, she arranges to marry Marcian, a general of stellar reputation, who agrees to respect his wife's vow of virginity. The two see eye to eye on politics, both civil and ecclesiastical. Moving swiftly to deal with the divisive effects of the Robber Council, the royal couple calls another general council.

Meanwhile the Huns threaten to invade, and Marcian hastens to the battlefield to take personal charge. Pulcheria, no stranger to councils, handles the arrangements. She selects as the assembly hall the Basilica of St. Euphemia at Chalcedon (near the capital) both for its accommodating size and because she trusts in the protection of that female martyr.

On October 8, 451, more than five hundred bishops—representing all the provinces of the Eastern Empire as well as four legates from Rome—begin their work. Once the business of Eutyches and the scandalous situation surrounding the meeting in 449 is disposed of, the council proceeds with the task of defining the nature of Jesus Christ—a doctrine still standing more than fifteen hundred years later. The definition, based on a letter written by Pope Leo, explains how Jesus' two distinct natures, human and divine, exist in one person.

When Marcian, back from the battlefield, appears before the bishops with Pulcheria, the two are acclaimed. She receives additional praise from the pope for being instrumental in restoring harmony to the church.

AFTERWARD

Following her death two years later, all of Pulcheria's personal wealth was distributed to the poor in accordance with her wishes. Her legacy to the bishop of Rome was beyond price. Through her efforts she had helped preserve mainstream Christianity, and by the use of Pope Leo's "Toma" (letter) as basis for the doctrine of Christ's nature, strengthened his position. Over a period of several years the pope had corresponded with Pulcheria about church matters. In one letter he wrote: "It was your care which brought to light the things contrived by the Devil through Eutyches; you must know that the whole Church of Rome is filled with joy through the workings of your faith, seen everywhere."[1]

In the past, rivalry among the patriarchates of Alexandria, Antioch, Constantinople, Jerusalem and Rome had been intense as they jousted for lead positions in the church. Two chief power centers emerged from Chalcedon: Constantinople and Rome. But the patriarchate of the former was destined to become more and more a political tool (future sovereigns would not be so dedicated as Pulcheria), and so its ecclesiastical strength was diluted.

In the West, a series of invasions by various tribes throughout much of the fifth century culminated in the deposing of the last Roman emperor in 476 by a Gothic chief named Odoacer. He was also, ironically, an officer in the imperial guard. (The Roman army by now was filled with recruits from Germanic tribes who had settled within the borders of the empire.) After that, the church remained the only institution left to help civilization on the continent survive a centuries-long period often marked by chaos as well as general cultural decline. (The previous expression, "Dark Ages," is no longer in use by historians, who view the era as much more complex. "Early Middle Ages" is now the preferred term.) As the only figure of authority, the head of the church in Rome out of necessity assumed temporal as well as

WOMEN IN CHURCH HISTORY

ecclesiastical rule. The papacy, in terms of authentic power, is sometimes said to have begun with Pope Leo.

One sad footnote to Chalcedon: Not everyone accepted the council's declarations. Among those refusing was the Egyptian church. Part of the problem stemmed from a misunderstanding caused by language differences. Some of the resistance also had to do with nationalistic feelings. Egyptians resented having to be subservient to foreign rule—that is, Constantinople— because the Byzantine Empire, as it was now being called, still held sway over Egypt.

INFINITE MAJESTY,

AMID THE BUSYNESS OF THE PALACE,
PULCHERIA CREATED A HOLY PLACE,
RULING HER DOMAIN
WITH WISDOM WROUGHT
FROM A STRONG FOUNDATION.

WE EACH NEED HOLY SPACE
FOR OUR OWN SANCTUARY,
IF NOT IN A BUILDING,
IN THE SOLITUDE OF OUR HEART.
AMEN.

THE SIXTH CENTURY

BRIGID OF KILDARE

BACKGROUND

Around the time that Saint Patrick was growing up in Britain, the last of the Roman legions departed its soil. Rome could no longer afford the expense of defending the far reaches of the empire. At age sixteen, Patrick left Britain too, though not willingly. His native Britons, representing what Christianity existed, lived in the interior—pushed there by invading Angles, Saxons and Jutes from northern Europe. Patrick was carried off by raiders to be sold as a slave to an Irish master; he worked in Ireland as a shepherd for six years before making his escape. Though much of Patrick's life is wrapped in legend, it appears that once free he decided to be a priest like his grandfather.

After training for Holy Orders in Gaul (France), Patrick chose to return to Ireland, this time as a missionary. Owing to the admirable Irish tolerance of new ideas, even religious ones, missionaries to that country never seemed to be candidates for martyrdom. When Patrick appeared on the scene in 432, there were already traces of Christianity. With his knowledge of the language and culture, along with a gift of persuasion, he made great headway. It has been suggested by some scholars who see similarities in religious practices that Egyptian monks may have made missionary journeys to this far western end of Europe. It's also been said that Ireland, until then having escaped any large-scale invasions, was not conquered until the Irish surrendered to Christianity.

KILDARE, IRELAND, C. 500

Brigid, abbess of a flourishing monastery in the valley of the River Liffey, decides she needs help and invites her friend Conleth to join her. With a group of followers, he has been leading an ascetic life in the neighborhood. Brigid convinces him to accept consecration as a bishop so that he can provide her establishment with the ecclesiastical services only a bishop can give. Conleth and his monks move to a site adjacent to her convent, creating a double monastery, the only known example in Ireland.

Brigid's power of persuasion had become evident early in life—a life that began about the year 450 in a place called Faughart on the east coast of Ireland. Her father, Dubtach, was chieftain of one of the country's numerous petty kingdoms, and her mother, Brocseach, served as a slave in his household.

When Dubtach's jealous wife insisted that he get rid of Brocseach, she was sold to a Druid who lived on the other side of the country. A Christian like her mother, Brigid spent her early years in the home of a pagan priest. Although the Irish were turning increasingly to the Christian faith, the Druid religion still claimed many adherents—Brigid's father among them.

At about age ten Brigid decided to return to her father's home, where she promptly upset the household with an unbreakable habit of giving away food, clothing and other family goods to the poor.

One day after getting word that her mother was ailing and could use a hand with the work, Brigid crossed back to the opposite coast, apparently not bothering to obtain her father's permission. Once more with the Druids, this time as a dairymaid, she continued to be as bountiful as ever, dispensing the master's butter, milk and cheese to the needy. But the girl's winning personality combined with her industriousness seemed to keep the master from despairing over her liberality.

In the meantime, despite Brigid's unconventional ways, her father had not given up on her. When she reached marriageable age, Dubtach went to great lengths to find exactly the right man for her. Extolling her assets—health, beauty, intelligence and a willingness to work—he produced a youth not only of exemplary character but, even more praiseworthy, a poet. At this time the bard enjoyed an exalted position in Irish society. Brigid would have lacked for nothing, including prestige. But the strong-willed young woman refused. Chieftain her father might be, but he was powerless when she overruled him.

While Dubtach aimed high for his natural daughter, her aim was higher: "Since I first fixed my mind on God," she once said, "I have never taken it off."[1] Regardless of the fact that no convents existed for women, Brigid decided to consecrate her life to God. (There had been monastic settlements for men since before Patrick's recent missionary endeavors.)

True to character, once Brigid had a dream, she wasted no time in making it become reality. First, though, came the matter of her mother's circumstances. As a woman in bondage, Brocseach possessed no rights. A slave is the property of the master who owns her, body and soul. But the resourceful Brigid, capitalizing on the fact that to give slaves their freedom is considered a magnanimous act, convinced the Druid master to set Brocseach free. Once she had her mother situated more favorably, Brigid was free to proceed with plans for her own future.

In Irish society then women desiring to live as consecrated virgins did so at home, devoting their days to prayer, works of mercy and the weaving of vestments and altar cloths. Families, especially those not Christian, often failed to understand, which made the life difficult.

Brigid found seven women of like mind, and together they approached a bishop named Maccaile, who agreed to accept their vows as nuns. Brigid and companions, dressed in simple white habits, made their profession about 469 in a ceremony at Westmeath, in the Midlands of Ireland. Bishop Maccaile draped a white cloak about Brigid's shoulders and a white veil on her "yellow locks," as tradition describes her hair. Ignoring her youthful age, he authorized Brigid to head Ireland's first convent. The site for it, his gift, was at a place called Croghan Hill.

For her part, Brigid had to see to the actual building of the convent. In religious settlements in the country, living space for community members typically consisted of a series of "cells." The cells, or huts, generally of clay and wattle, were constructed in the shape of a beehive—perfect for shedding rain in the moist climate. The earthen floors were strewn with rushes to ensure both warmth and cleanliness. (Examples of the beehive hut are still to be seen.) Even the church—though the main building—was ordinarily of modest proportions and built of wood. The whole was then enclosed by walls of earth or stone, much as Irish chieftains designed their fortress-headquarters.

Once settled in, the nuns did not settle back, for a monastic colony is meant to be self-supporting as well as prayer-filled. The women farmed the fields surrounding the enclosure, and when that work was done they kept occupied with spinning and embroidery. (The Irish prized handwork of all kinds.) In addition, the convent offered asylum to anyone in need.

Brigid and the seven other nuns—who seem to have remained lifelong, loyal companions—soon found that more cells must be added to accommodate others desirous of this new and stimulating kind of life where holiness can be developed along with a woman's talents.

Once the pioneering monastery is in full swing and running smoothly, Brigid eagerly goes about the business of setting up similar foundations in other parts of Ireland. With a nun or two to accompany her, she begins to journey the length and breadth of the country: crossing rivers, meadows and bogs, traveling roads that are little more than a track. The usual transportation, a two-horse chariot, is driven either by a laborer in her employ or sometimes by the chaplain of one of her settlements, though she can handle the chariot, too.

She sees her apostolic work well-rewarded as the land blossoms with new communities for women. Just as Patrick before her had attracted converts and encouraged the founding of monasteries (though only for men), Brigid, too, enjoys the gift of drawing people to herself. (Whether the two ever met is debatable, since Patrick died when she was still a child.)

Christianity's appeal to the Irish may be owed not only to a natural fervor but also to an inherent love of learning. In the "colleges" of Celtic tradition, poets might spend a dozen years in disciplined study of the extensive, rich Celtic literature in oral form. Patrick had brought with him on the missionary trail a written language using the Latin alphabet. This contribution to his adopted land, whose heritage included a reverence for words, was a treasure indeed.

Happily, the Christianized chieftains donate land for church use, and as monastic colonies flourish, so, too, does their growing reputation as centers of learning. Women as well as men participate in this outburst of education, which is not limited to study of Scripture and the church fathers. For the converted Irish never turn their backs on their native culture; they preserve the best. Neither do they neglect the secular classics of Western civilization.

At the same time, Europe's troubles are multiplying due to invasions and mass migrations of Goths, Vandals and other tribes. For safety's sake, monks flee the continent to Ireland, bringing with them irreplaceable manuscripts from their monasteries and valuable pieces of art, too.

The Irish set about creating some great art of their own as well. Brigid's premier foundation at Kildare, for instance, specializes in the production of manuscripts. In the scriptorium, nuns and monks illuminate parchment pages with superb illustrations, border designs and richly decorative capital letters—all done in sumptuous colors and gold leaf. In order to preserve learning, they laboriously copy by hand page after page of academic and religious texts.

While today the eighth-century *Book of Kells*, an illuminated manuscript of the Gospels enshrined in a Dublin library, is considered possibly the most beautiful such work in the world, it was preceded by the *Book of Kildare*. Seen as late as the twelfth century by a historian whose description makes it comparable to Kells, the Kildare example disappeared during the English invasion in that same century. That historian, Giraldus Cambrensis, describes it thus: "...you will be able to observe intricacies so delicate and ingenious, so strict and artful, so involved and interlaced, and illuminated with colours still so fresh, that verily you would say these were all combined by the diligence of an angel rather than of a man. For my part, the more often and carefully I look upon it, I am ever astonished anew: I ever find food for wonder."[2]

Kildare began simply enough. Brigid started with her own oratory, or place of prayer, a cell built under an oak tree (*"Cill-Dara"*) in what had been a pagan sanctuary. (The Druid faith centered on nature worship, making temples unnecessary. This may explain the simplicity of religious architecture in Irish tradition.)

By the time Brigid invites Conleth to become a bishop and share jurisdiction with her at Kildare, the monastic village has assumed the proportions of a city. There are blacksmiths, carpenters, a granary and all else needed to be self-sufficient.

Conleth, before taking up the religious life, had been a metalworker, and this craft is added to Kildare's other artistic endeavors. The monastery produces church bells, chalices, crosiers and other liturgical objects for Ireland's burgeoning churches and monasteries.

Even with expansion, churches such as the one at Kildare continue to be built in the plain, timbered style, though interiors are hung with rich tapestries and the walls covered with frescoes. Down the center of the Kildare nave, a screen divides monks from nuns. In the daily tasks they might work side by side, but when it comes to worship, they pray separately.

In Brigid's day the monastery serves as ecclesiastical base for the Irish church rather than the diocese, as elsewhere in Europe, where it is headquartered in a city. Ireland as yet has no cities. As a result, power is centered in the abbot and abbess instead of the bishop. (The diocesan structure was patterned after a standard unit of Roman government. Ireland, having escaped occupation by Roman legions, lacks that model. It seems logical to follow their own social order, based on tribal divisions.)

Attached to the churches of major monasteries are what become known as "cathedral schools." Many of the schools come to number nearly a thousand students, who might lodge at the monastery if room is available, or in nearby houses, free of charge. But generally they build huts for themselves in the neighborhood. Kildare's, an important school, attracts students and scholars from all parts of Europe with a curriculum encompassing the seven liberal arts as well as religious studies.

With all the activity of Kildare and her other communities, Brigid still aids the needy, though her unbounded charity at times upsets even her nuns. She also entertains a constant stream of visitors. All guests are treated alike—whether bishop, chieftain or leper. When a feast day nears, she does not find it beneath her dignity to brew ale for the occasion. Some visitors come for the hospitality, others for advice. Finian, for example, learns from Brigid how to organize a monastery before building his celebrated one at Clonard.

As Mother Abbess of all Ireland's convents, Brigid knows well how to exercise authority, for part of her background is royal, her inheritance from Dubtach. But she never forgets what it was like to be on the low end of the social scale in the Druid's dairy. To the end of her long and healthy life, Brigid can be found milking cows, making butter and cheese and laboring in the fields, singing as she does so, for music gives her great pleasure. In the solitude of meadow, sky and fresh air she nourishes her spirit.

Many are the whimsical stories the Irish like to tell of Brigid, the classic one being the time she dried her wet cloak on a sunbeam. The searcher after her very real contributions to Christianity and the church may grow frustrated over the recital of impossible-sounding tales. Yet in the end it becomes apparent that the poetic parable tells the most important truth about this exuberant Irish saint: Authentic holiness wears the face of joy.

AFTERWARD

Brigid's gifts to the Christian world include helping establish the foundations of education for the laity through monastery schools, which developed into the universities of the Middle Ages. Moreover, she gave the women of her country the opportunity to use their energies and intellect in a way previously not open to them. For many generations after her, Kildare would continue to be ruled by a double line of abbesses and abbot-bishops. Only in medieval times were convents placed entirely under the jurisdiction of men.

The abbesses and abbots of Brigid's era laid the foundation for Ireland's Golden Age—the centuries in which it remained a beacon of light while the continent experienced social stagnation and frequent chaos. The Irish produced a new flowering of scholars, well-rounded, intellectually tolerant, "unfettered minds," in one writer's words. At the same time they pursued the ascetic life, though they didn't talk about their heroic penances, only performing them—ascetics with a smile! When Irish missionaries began going to England, Scotland and the continent, they took along the special brand of enthusiastic piety.

Late in the eighth century, Irish monastic culture fell victim to Viking raids; monasteries were plundered and burned. Even so, until the twelfth-century invasion by England and the crushing occupation which followed, Gaelic culture was regarded as one of the most advanced in Europe.

LORD JESUS,

ONE CAN PICTURE BRIGID
SINGING AND REJOICING
AS SHE EMPTIES THE LARDER
FOR SOMEONE IN NEED,
NEVER MIND THE COST.

CHRISTIAN LOVE, NOT DUTY,
MAKES THE WORLD GO ROUND.
A GLADSOME GIVER—
LET IT BE SAID OF ME.
AMEN.

THE SEVENTH CENTURY

Hilda of Whitby

Background

Not all waves of conversions occurred through the efforts of vowed missionaries. Women of royalty often played an influential role. For example, in the waning years of the fifth century, Clovis, king of the Franks, had accepted baptism in response to the promptings of his wife, the devout Queen Clotilde. This added considerably to the domain of Christianity, since Clovis's kingdom eventually included most of territorial France as well as southwest Germany. The first Frankish ruler to convert, he set a precedent for future kings in the West by becoming a defender of Christianity. Needless to say, his nobility found it advisable to follow him to the baptistery, as eventually did most of his other subjects.

Women of royal blood set another trend: becoming nuns and founding their own religious communities. The first to do so was

Radegund, another Frankish queen, around the middle of the sixth century. Forced into marriage, she managed to escape the unhappy situation and went on to establish an abbey at Poitiers in west central France. Her abbey was the original of the great double monasteries to flourish in her country.

Following the pattern set earlier, Bertha, the Christian daughter of the king of Paris, crossed the channel to wed the pagan King Ethelbert of Kent, who was ruler of all southern England. She brought with her a bishop as her chaplain. Meanwhile, Pope Gregory I sent missionaries to Ethelbert's domain, and they were warmly received. After Ethelbert's baptism in 597, Pope Gregory wrote to Queen Bertha, saying that she more than anyone else was responsible for the conversions that resulted.

Incidentally, the first convent in England was founded in Folkestone in 630 by a subsequent king of Kent for his daughter Eanswythe, honored as England's first nun. Since rebuilt, the church he erected for her—and bearing her name—is the pride of today's Folkestone.

YORK, KINGDOM OF NORTHUMBRIA, 627

According to the *Anglo-Saxon Chronicle*, King Edwin was baptized at Easter, along with many of his people, by Paulinus.

In this essentially pagan land, when the king decides to convert to Christianity, the court as well as a number of his subjects do likewise. The occasion comes about as a result of the arrival two years before of Edwin's Christian bride, Ethelberga of Kent (daughter of Bertha) and her chaplain Paulinus. He had been among the missionaries sent to Kent from Rome several decades earlier. (Though Christianity had reached England with the Roman legions, it never became widespread.)

Paulinus, now bishop, performs the multiple baptisms in the "cathedral," a small wooden church. One of his new converts is a thirteen-year-old great-niece of the king named Hilda.

When she was just a baby, her father was banished by another king and died in exile of poisoning. The girl has since been reared at court. History mentions her mother only in reference to Hilda's infancy.

These are turbulent, sometimes savage times as the leaders of rival kingdoms in England wage war against each other for territorial supremacy. When Edwin is killed in battle, the Northumbrian throne falls to men who are still pagans. The queen and her small children, with Bishop Paulinus as escort, flee to the safety of Christian Kent, never to return. Hilda remains, however, for her roots are in the north.

Within a few years, the throne is regained by a genuinely devout Christian. The new King Oswald, who had been in exile at Iona, an island off the western coast of Scotland, invites monks from that Irish missionary base to evangelize his kingdom. They respond by establishing churches and schools, using as their center another island, Lindisfarne, this one not far from the king's court on the northeastern coast of England.

When Oswald is killed in battle, fighting over the throne resumes. The constant strife may explain why Hilda, now thirty-three and feeling the call to be a nun, decides to join her sister in a convent near Paris. Of noble birth and well-educated, Hilda might have married had there been parents to arrange it. Perhaps she feels lucky simply not to have been carried off as part of the spoils of war, as so often happens to women of her time.

In 647 she travels down to East Anglia, where her widowed sister's son is king, and stays at his court while awaiting passage to France. During her prolonged wait for a ship, the Irish missionary Bishop Aidan arrives in East Anglia to seek her assistance. He wants to resume his work in Northumbria, which was interrupted by the fighting. With the situation calm once more, he persuades her to return.

His idea is that Hilda help him develop the monastic life according to the Irish approach: combining scholarship with holiness. He gives her a small piece of land by the River Wear, where she and a few friends of similar inclination take up residence, spending a quiet year in prayer. The end of that period coincides with the departure of the founder-abbess of Hartlepool, on the North Sea coast. That abbess had been the first nun in Northumbria, consecrated about 640 by Bishop Aidan.

As new abbess of the Hartlepool convent, Hilda perfects the methods of organization and discipline that will prepare her for the important work in her future. Even now she earns the high regard of Aidan and other men of religion.

The story of her eight years at Hartlepool is recounted in Bede's *Ecclesiastical History of the English People*. Bede, a monk born in 643, spent all his life in Northumbria and knew some of Hilda's contemporaries. The monk writes of her "innate wisdom, and inclination to the service of God," reporting that not only ordinary people "but even kings and princes, as occasion offered, asked and received her advice." Hilda directs her nuns in a life marked by "strict observance of justice, piety, and chastity, and other virtues, and particularly of peace and charity...."[1]

Oswy, the current king, wins a decisive victory over the pagan leader of a rival kingdom. Having vowed to consecrate his baby daughter Elfleda to God in return for victory, he entrusts her to Hilda's care. With the baby goes a dowry of sorts: "twelve estates." The extensive piece of property apparently includes the site known then by the Old English name Streaneshalch (translated "Lighthouse Bay"), but more familiar to history by its later name: Whitby.

In 657 Hilda supervises the building at Whitby of a double monastery to house monks and nuns—a common arrangement for early English monasteries. The setting, about thirty miles down the coast from Hartlepool, is unusually dramatic: on a headland three hundred feet above the bay, where the River Esk empties into the North Sea. From the commanding hilltop can be seen the surrounding moors as well as the ocean.

The complex of buildings making up a convent for nuns and an abbey for monks are of austerely plain construction, similar to the monastic settlements of Ireland. (Hilda's mentor, Aidan, has since died, to be succeeded by another Irishman, Finian.)

With the completion of the monastery, the nuns and monks elect Hilda their superior. Under her direction Whitby becomes famous as a center of holiness and scholarship. Like the communities of primitive Christianity, the monks and nuns hold all goods in common, with no separation of classes into rich and poor. (Monasteries on the continent cannot always make this claim.) The hundreds of religious who come under Hilda's supervision spend countless hours studying, copying by hand the Bible and other great books, translating and illuminating manuscripts. In fact, the Whitby library becomes known as one of England's finest.

The abbess also attaches a school to the complex which attracts scholars from other countries. In this environment, there are master instructors for all who pursue the study of Holy Scripture. Music has a role in the cultured atmosphere, too, and almost everyone in the monastery can play the harp or another instrument.

Hilda's spiritual and intellectual guidance eventually results in five of her monks being raised to the episcopacy, and Whitby's reputation is such that bishops look to it as their source for clergymen.

The indefatigable abbess also attends to the welfare of laypersons living in the area overseen by her monastery (for abbesses of Hilda's rank maintained a major say in the administration of wide territories). On the grounds itself is a house for the sick.

Looked on as the most learned woman in England of her time, she appears to enjoy most nurturing or fostering the gifts of others, whether it be the training of future bishops or future poets. Again from Bede: "all that knew her called [her] Mother, for her singular piety and grace."[2]

One day Hilda happens to hear that an illiterate cowherd employed at Whitby shows an unusual talent for song. She calls Caedmon in, recognizes his poetic ability, persuades him to leave the tending of cows to others and invites him to join the religious community. Given instruction in Scripture, Caedmon composes songs in the vernacular, using words easily memorized in order to make stories of the faith understandable and interesting for the common people—a need Hilda clearly recognizes. For example, he describes creation in this verse:

First, for a roof,
O'er the children of earth,
He stablished the heavens,
And founded the world,
And spread the dry land
For the living to dwell in.
Lord Everlasting!
Almighty God![3]

Ultimately, Caedmon will achieve fame as England's first Christian poet.

An age when both the northern and southern kingdoms are primarily Christian ought to be peaceful. For when King Oswy defeated his pagan adversary, it meant the collapse of the last pagan stronghold—one that had occupied the heartland of England. In a sense though, the pagan section so strategically located had served as a sort of buffer between the Celtic- or Irish-oriented church of the north and the Rome-dominated church of the south.

The two differed chiefly in this respect: A Roman-style institution emphasized a hierarchical structure and strict conformance in thought and ritual, while the Irish favored a free-spirited approach that resulted in independence of thought and a lack of centralization. The inevitable clash will come about over a seemingly trivial matter.

King Oswy is accustomed to the Celtic tradition brought and sustained by dedicated Irish missionaries. But his wife Eanfleda is from Kent, the kingdom converted by missionaries from Rome. Though nothing so serious as doctrinal differences exist, practices vary. Chief among them is the date Easter is celebrated.

A century or two earlier, Rome had revised the system of determining the date, but the Celtic church stayed with the old way. Things came to a head: "when the king having ended the time of fasting, kept his Easter, the queen and her followers were still fasting, and celebrating Palm Sunday."[4] This put the entire court in a quandary, uncertain which member of the royal couple to follow.

On a lesser scale but of concern to the monks is the tonsure, the direction in which their heads were shaved. The Celts shaved the front of the head from ear to ear, leaving the hair on the back of the head to grow long. With the Roman tonsure, all hair is shaved except for a ring encircling the head. The younger monks grow increasingly resentful over the difference.

These somewhat mild issues mask the underlying one: Which party will prevail—Celtic or Roman? The future of the English church depended on the outcome. To resolve the impasse, a synod is called in 664 and Whitby, because of its prestige, is chosen as the meeting place under the presidency of its abbess.

An abbot from each side presents his case before the king, who sits as judge. Oswy's natural sympathy favors the Celtic cause, but as he listens, he is won over by the argument that Rome has inherited the keys of the kingdom directly from Peter. That's enough for Oswy. He cannot, will not, contradict Peter.

Hilda, too, leans toward the Irish side, for her mentors were from that background, but she yields for the sake of peace. Harmony in the English church (with a few exceptions) is preserved, and the unity of Western Christendom strengthened.

Hilda goes on governing the monastery even though, in her last seven years, she suffers from ill health. Ever a lover of peace, in her final words to the community "she admonished them to preserve evangelical peace among themselves, and with all others."[5]

AFTERWARD

The king's baby daughter Elfleda, who had been entrusted to Hilda's care, grew up to become Hilda's successor as head of Whitby. Women played a prominent role in Anglo-Saxon society, including participation in the intellectual renaissance that began in Hilda's time.

The tradition developed in English monasteries and the schools associated with them were characterized by discipline, a sense of stability and a high standard of scholarship. Many religious centers became famous for their learning.

Long before becoming one politically, England achieved religious unity, thanks to the Whitby synod. This brought its church into closer contact with the church on the continent. Bridging the two would have enormous impact in the following century, when English missionaries took their monastic tradition abroad. This included a passion for learning inherited from the Irish and organizational skills which came to them by way of Rome—a combination of qualities that practically ensure success in mission lands. As an added bonus, England provided Charlemagne with an outstanding scholar to direct his palace school: Alcuin, a Northumbrian-educated monk, who helped spark the Carolingian Renaissance.

GOOD AND WISE SHEPHERD,

WHETHER BISHOPS OR COWHERDS,
THEY CALLED HER MOTHER,
FOR HILDA NURTURED ALL
TO BECOME WHAT GOD
MEANT THEM TO BE.

AN ENCOURAGING WORD,
A HELPFUL DEED,
THUS LITTLE BY LITTLE
WILL MY "CHILDREN" BLOSSOM,
AMEN.

7 : HILDA OF WHITBY

THE EIGHTH CENTURY

LIOBA, ANGLO-SAXON MISSIONARY TO GERMANY

BACKGROUND

In the first decade or so of the eighth century, the once-flourishing church in North Africa was overrun by Muslims. The faithful in Egypt soon became a minority, while the armies of Islam embarked on the conquest of Spain. Their advance into Europe was not halted until a defeat by Charles Martel (grandfather of Charlemagne) at Poitiers in 732.

At the eastern end of the Mediterranean, though Constantinople was so far spared, the constant threat of Islam affected policies. At various times Byzantine emperors used the issue of iconoclasm (destruction of holy images) to assert their authority over both church and state. This controversy in the East over the veneration of icons or statues of Jesus, Mary and the saints—some called it idolatry—often erupted into violence not unlike that which occurred earlier with regard to the doctrine on the nature of Christ.

Along with many monks, women were especially prominent in the defense of icons. They had the support of the church in Rome. (Taking sides was to create enemies in the East for Rome.) The issue was not finally settled until a council in Constantinople, called by Empress Theodora II in 843, approved the veneration of icons.

Life was more peaceable in England, at least in monastic enclaves such as the one founded in 718 by Cuthburg, sister to a king. Her abbey at Wimborne in Wessex (the West Country) was free to grow and prosper in relative security. Even when Vikings began attacking England late in that century, the eastern coast bore the brunt.

Mainz, Germany, 748

In a letter to Tetta, abbess of the great English abbey at Wimborne, Boniface asks for assistance with his missionary work among the Frankish tribes of Germany. He specifically requests that his younger cousin Lioba be one of the nuns sent.

The two cousins had begun corresponding some time before that, starting with a letter written by Lioba, then a novice at the abbey in the southwest of England. Enclosing a gift of Latin verses, Lioba reminds Boniface of their family connection (on her mother's side). "I am their only daughter, and, unworthy as I am, I should be so happy if you would be to me as a brother. No man of our kindred gives me the confidence and hope which I find in you. I am sending you a little present, not because it is good enough, but that you may not forget me while you are far away.... I do so badly want to hear from you."[1]

Touched by what Lioba wrote, Boniface saved the letter and began the regular exchange that deepens their friendship in the ensuing years.

Boniface communicated with many people in England, and from them he heard praise for Lioba's learning and holiness, her willingness to do manual labor and her blithe young spirit. Surely she is missionary material. Still, he must also have had great confidence in her potential to survive in the heathen, primitive society of Germany—particularly in light of Lioba's sheltered and cultured background.

Born in Wessex of middle-aged parents whose hope for a baby was almost gone, she was so cherished they called her Lioba, meaning "the loved one." Wanting the best for their only child, they placed her in a monastery school, since it provided the best education for girls as well as boys. Upon coming of age, she decided to become a nun, a choice that in this instance entailed perpetual enclosure, with travel outside permitted under special circumstances. (Wimborne was a double monastery where Abbess Tetta ruled over both nuns and monks. There was no contact between members of the two communities, however.)

When Boniface sends for Lioba, she has become the novice mistress and one of the more promising members at Wimborne. Reluctantly, the abbess lets her go, along with a band of thirty other nuns, to set up a convent in the heartland of Germany.

Boniface knows full well the conditions the women must face, though the situation has improved since a papal commission first made him apostle to Germany. True, the church existed in this wilderness land prior to his arrival, but he found it in a pitiable state. Christian ritual mingled freely with pagan practices. Magic spells were common, and so was nature worship. Boniface had been appalled, as he wrote to Pope Zacharias in 742, to discover that deacons "have spent their lives since childhood in debauchery, adultery and every kind of uncleanness... and who even now, when they have four or five or even more concubines in their beds at night, are brazen enough to call themselves deacons and read out the Gospel."[2] Even worse, Boniface went on, they continued this lifestyle after becoming priests. Church reform was desperately needed.

He could not begin to think then of setting up religious communities of women. Now, after he has labored more than two decades to bring order, the time seems right.

Lioba and her companions arrive at Mainz after a fatiguing journey, first crossing the English Channel, then making their way by road and river to the monastery Boniface has ready for them. It is called Bischofsheim, or "Bishop's House," which suggests that he is turning over his own residence to the women. (Boniface had been consecrated a bishop while on a visit to Rome.)

He greets them warmly, especially pleased to meet his cousin Lioba—the one described as having "a face like an angel, ever pleasant and laughing."[3] He puts her in charge of the fledgling community, and this she will govern as abbess for the next twenty-eight years, though she also establishes elsewhere in Germany houses over which Boniface gives her authority.

The nuns are to follow the Benedictine Rule, as do Boniface's monks: combining manual labor with intellectual pursuits and observing moderation in all things rather than severe asceticism. Life in this wilderness land can be rough enough.

Boniface's aim for both nuns and monks is that they work to set up monasteries throughout the land—Christian centers to provide a civilizing influence. In the past, many in the Frankish kingdom converted out of loyalty to tribal chiefs. The net result was faith of only a superficial nature. To sink deep roots, religious education is called for; in the process, vocations can be drawn from the native population to ensure the future of the church.

Lioba's nuns assume the charge of educating Frankish girls. Their convent setting is a far cry from that of Wimborne Abbey, but wherever a colony of religious settle, the surrounding countryside undergoes a transformation. Clearing land for the planting of crops has the most visible effect. Additionally, no matter how makeshift the monastery buildings at first, the presence of holy men and women serves as a powerful antidote to the dark forces of paganism, which still maintain a stronghold (even human sacrifice occasionally occurs).

Typically, settlements of all kinds, whether secular or religious, are built on Germany's abundant waterways, for these prove by far the safest way to travel. Between the population centers come wide stretches of uncultivated forests without roads or, at best, with poorly marked ones. Brigands as well as wild animals pose dangers there.

Lioba and her nuns do more than teach, for every monastic settlement is also a place of refuge for the sick or hungry and a hospice for the traveler. Anyone who knocks at the door, even a criminal, must be welcomed and cared for. Because Frankish rulers provide no welfare for the needy, the church acts as protector. And the population suffers hardships aplenty: epidemics among livestock, plagues among people, famine, endless winters, floods. There is no technology to ease the problems of uncertain climate or disease—only the selfless efforts of nuns and monks.

In the face of all this, Lioba gives ample evidence of being a reassuring presence to the superstitious peasants. Her imperturbable calm becomes the stuff of legends. There is the time, for instance, that a fire breaks out in a nearby village, spreading rapidly from one thatched roof to the next. The fire grows to threaten even the monastery. In panic, the villagers rush to find the abbess. In her quiet yet practical way, Lioba directs them to take buckets from the river that flows past and throw water on the flames. When they follow her order, the flames are extinguished. "At this miracle," reports a monk named Rudolf, "the whole crowd stood amazed and broke out into the praise of God, who through the faith and prayers of his handmaid had delivered them so extraordinarily from a terrible danger."[4] (To Rudolf is owed the biography of Lioba, based on information he obtained from her contemporaries.)

On another occasion, during a fierce thunderstorm, the terror-stricken villagers take refuge in the church. Lioba invites them to pray with her, but they are too overcome with fear. As the storm continues unabated, she opens the church doors and "stretches out her hands to heaven and three times invokes the mercy of Christ," asking that "he would come quickly to the help of his people." Suddenly the storm dies away and the sun comes out.

Almost as fabled as her courage is Lioba's hospitality. According to Rudolf, "She kept open house for all without exception, and even when she was fasting gave banquets and washed the feet of the guests with her own hands, at once the guardian and the minister of the practice instituted by our Lord."[5]

Most days are spent more routinely, however, with the nuns dividing their days into prayer, study, teaching and manual work. The work may be in the bakehouse, the brewhouse or in performing household duties. A particular sphere of activity is the pro duction of books. The scriptorium keeps busy copying manuscripts to use in the training of future clergy and nuns.

Lioba is never without a book herself, continuing her own studies though already well-versed in the Old and New Testaments, the writings of the church fathers and canon law (the collection of laws governing church affairs). Neither are the liberal arts neglected. When the abbess lies down for the midday rest, the younger nuns take turns reading to her from Scripture. But even when she appears to be almost asleep, they dare not skip a word or she will immediately make a correction.

She encourages her nuns in scholarship. For example, Huneberc, an Anglo-Saxon nun at their convent in Heidenheim, writes an account of the monk Willibald's travels. (The two missionaries are good friends.) It is the only narrative in existence of an eighth-century pilgrimage to the Holy Land and also the earliest travel book by an English writer.

The women obviously regard their superior with great affection. The small cup from which the abstemious Lioba drinks is known as "the Beloved's little one." And to Boniface she is the "dear one," for as they work closely together, the bonds of friendship grow stronger.

When he prepares to leave for the dangerous mission field of Frisia (part of the Netherlands) to preach to its pagans, perhaps he has a premonition of the martyrdom that awaits him there, for he asks Lioba to meet him at his headquarters in Mainz prior to departure. Maybe Boniface recalls his cousin's earlier gift of Latin verses that he might not forget her while far away. As a parting gift—to remember him by—he presents his "dear one" with his monk's cowl.

Then, calling together his senior monks, Boniface reaffirms a wish made previously: that after death, he and Lioba should be laid to rest in the same tomb at Fulda, his favorite monastery. He explains why: "that we who in this life together have served Christ with the same devotion and love, may together await the day of resurrection."[6]

In the long years following Boniface's martyrdom in Frisia, Lioba, though admittedly lonely, continues the apostolic work the two once shared. Her closest friend during this latter stage of her life is Hildegard, wife of Charlemagne (who in 771 became sole ruler of the Franks). Much as Lioba dislikes the hectic atmosphere of the royal court at Aachen, for the sake of their friendship she sometimes will accept Hildegard's insistent invitations. There,

Rudolf writes, "The princes loved her, the nobles received her, the bishops welcomed her with joy. And because of her wide knowledge of the Scriptures and her prudence in counsel they often discussed spiritual matters and ecclesiastical discipline with her."[7]

At other times Lioba visits the various convents around Germany to monitor their progress. What she likes best, though, is going to Fulda to pray at the tomb of Boniface—a privilege denied all other women, for entrance to the monastery is forbidden to them. (Boniface in his lifetime had granted her the favor of praying at Fulda.)

In her final years Lioba retires to a small convent four miles south of Mainz, where she spends her days in fasting and prayer. Upon her death in 780, the monks at Fulda decide against carrying out Boniface's last request, seeing it somehow as an impropriety. They elect instead to bury her at Fulda, but in a tomb apart from her cousin's.

AFTERWARD

History regards the missionary endeavors of Boniface, Lioba and company in Germany as the most important apostolic work of the eighth century. The immediate results were beneficial enough: a civilizing effect on a primitive society and education as a weapon in the struggle to survive a hostile environment. Wherever religious settlements were founded, monks and nuns cleared and cultivated the surrounding wilderness and passed on more advanced agricultural techniques to their German neighbors.

Through their promotion of learning and the arts, monks and nuns helped lay the groundwork for the Carolingian Renaissance. Some say the spread of monasteries had a more lasting impact on Europe than Charlemagne's empire building. (Boniface's and Lioba's way of evangelizing was in marked contrast to Charlemagne's, who was inclined to make wholesale conversions at the point of a sword.)

In the long term, bringing Christian civilization to the heart-land of Europe was crucial to the continent's historical development. As the various Frankish tribes united in a common religion, the Holy Roman Empire emerged. In that empire, too, several centuries later, the convents Lioba established would play a role, still bearing fruit as a new renaissance came about.

LAMB OF GOD,

LITTLE DID LIOBA KNOW
WHEN SHE OFFERED THE GIFT OF FRIENDSHIP,
IT WOULD TAKE HER TO A LAND
UNLIKE ANYTHING SHE'D KNOWN BEFORE:
ADVENTURE-FILLED.

DARE I STRAY BEYOND
A COMFORTABLE CIRCLE OF FRIENDS?
WHO STANDS OUTSIDE THAT CIRCLE,
WAITING FOR MY OUTSTRETCHED HAND?
AMEN.

THE NINTH CENTURY

LUDMILA OF BOHEMIA

BACKGROUND

The Carolingian dynasty, founded in the seventh century, reached its zenith when Charlemagne was crowned emperor of the West by Pope Leo III on Christmas Day, 800. On the throne in the East, the Empress Irene not only disliked the idea of a rival power, but also scoffed at that "barbarian" from a Frankish tribe brazen enough to seek such an honored position. (She sat on the throne at Constantinople as a result of having first discredited the heir, her son, then having him blinded.)

Neither the Carolingians nor the Byzantines could measure up to the two magnificent civilizations contemporary with their times. In China the T'ang dynasty was creating a dazzling array of works of art, poetry and scientific developments such as the printing press (which was not seen in Europe until centuries later). And in Baghdad, the Abbasid dynasty reflected Arab achievements of like brilliance in an empire stretching from the borders of India to the Iberian Peninsula.

Though unheralded, in a remote corner of Europe there quietly sprang up a dynasty destined to add luster to the honor roll of saints. As tradition tells it, a Bohemian queen, Libussa, married a peasant named Premysl at an unknown date in the eighth century. The marriage gave birth to the Premyslide dynasty, which eventually united the Slavic settlements of Bohemia into a single duchy.

DUCHY OF BOHEMIA, C. 880

The first Christians to be converted in their land, Duke Borivoy and his wife Ludmila (daughter of a Slav prince), show enthusiasm for their new faith by building Bohemia's first church at the site of the royal residence north of Prague. They dedicate it to Saint Clement, an esteemed pope and martyr of the first century.

As ruler of the duchy (part of today's Czech Republic), Borivoy attempts to impose Christianity on the pagan population but meets with stiff resistance, particularly from the leading families and the pagan priests. The latter's power is extensive enough to control the justice system, administering the laws of the land. Though in its primitive form the Slavic religion revolves around vague spirits of nature, where life is more developed (as in Prague), there are deities representing the forces of good and evil, temples and a hierarchy of priests.

While it may be common practice for monarchs to enforce their own religious beliefs on the people, in this case the opposition proves too strong. When an uprising begins, Borivoy and Ludmila flee east to the court of the Moravian prince for protection until order can be restored.

Order returns only after the leader of the rebellion is killed. Home again, the royal couple builds its next church on Castle Hill in Prague, near an old heathen place of sacrifice, and dedicate it to the Virgin Mary. But they otherwise tread more lightly in conversion attempts, for the native religion remains thoroughly entrenched. (Although in 845, German missionaries in the wider region had baptized fourteen princes and their households—the earliest recorded baptisms in Czech history—nothing further seems to have come of that episode.)

The next set of missionaries to Slavic lands (Slav tribes inhabited much of eastern Europe) would come by invitation of the Moravian kingdom, Bohemia's neighbor to the east. Because only a short time has elapsed since Moravia won back independence from Charlemagne's heirs, the prince fears German missionaries would have too much influence. Wanting Christianity for his kingdom but not Germanic rule again, he asks the Byzantine emperor at Constantinople to dispatch missionaries from the eastern half of the church. (The formal break between the patriarch at Constantinople and the pope at Rome has yet to come, though the rivalry is heating up.)

Two monks, Cyril and Methodius, accept the invitation and meet with immediate success in Moravia, for the two, having mastered the Slavic language, preach and conduct the liturgy in the vernacular. When the pope learns of this, he summons the monks to Rome, hears their case, then gives permission to continue use of the Slavic language at Mass. Cyril's death occurs in 869, while Methodius, responsible for baptizing Borivoy and Ludmila, dies in 884.

These are turbulent times everywhere in Europe. Charlemagne's successors are battling over who is to rule which territory; the Magyars, a tribe out of Asia, conduct a roving war on horseback; Vikings and Saracens invade different parts of the continent; and the papacy is in a vastly weakened condition. (About the time of Ludmila's baptism the only strong pope of the ninth century was hammered to death by his own relatives.)

In the meantime, Ludmila gives birth to two sons, while Borivoy is occupied with political struggles. Despite Bohemia's geographical location as a frontier land, its major town, Prague, is far from a backwater in commercial terms. The castle, in fact, is a fortification that protects Prague's growing position as a trade center. Its greatest asset is the Moldau River, which flows the entire length of the country, connecting in the north with a German waterway. In consequence, Prague serves as crossroads for the lucrative European routes, both north-south and east-west.

When Borivoy dies in 895 at the age of thirty-five, his two sons, barely of age to govern, succeed him as joint rulers. Their mother remains in the background, quietly but steadfastly working in behalf of Christianity.

When the first grandson is born, her son Ratislav and daughter-in-law Drahomira entrust Ludmila with the child's upbringing. Her chaplain, Paul of Ancona, who had been a personal disciple of Methodius, baptizes the baby Wenceslaus and later helps with the boy's education. He and Ludmila, of considerable learning herself, teach Wenceslaus to read Latin as well as Slavic and train him to abide by the highest moral principles.

When Wenceslaus's father dies while fighting the Magyars (Ludmila's other son was killed earlier), the forceful and ambitious Drahomira assumes the regency, for her son has not yet attained his majority. Until now Christianity has been making slow gains, but Drahomira, who is no more than a nominal believer, becomes a willing tool of the anti-Christian party. The nobility belonging to it encourage her jealousy of Ludmila's influence on Wenceslaus, and Drahomira promptly removes the young man from his grandmother's care. Only in secret will he be able to worship or to see his Christian friends.

The new regent also issues in strictest terms an order forbidding priests and others who profess Christianity to instruct children. She removes Christian magistrates installed previously by either Duke Borivoy or one of his sons and replaces them with followers of paganism. Drahomira suspects—true or not—that her mother-in-law may be trying to persuade Wenceslaus to take the reins of government before he comes of ruling age. The popular young man could rally the citizenry to his side and thus save the faith. Ludmila herself, because of an inherent gentleness and charity, is greatly loved by the Bohemian people. (Interestingly, Ludmila's name in Slavic means "people's love.")

Drahomira's suspicions are further fed by tales concocted by the anti-Christian faction. Though no one knows for certain if the regent had any role in the murder plot, two nobles of the pagan party go to the Castle of Tetin outside of Prague, where Ludmila is spending her "retirement." There, on September 16, 921, they strangle her while she is at prayer in the chapel. She thus becomes Bohemia's first martyr.

AFTERWARD

Shortly after, Drahomira, in political maneuvering to aid enemies of the German king, gets into trouble and is banished from the court. Wenceslaus is proclaimed ruler. He negotiates peace with the invading Germans, initiating a policy of friendly relations with them, seeing that as the wisest course to deal with a more powerful neighbor (though it offends national pride). He then strives to strengthen Christianity in his kingdom. Neither policy sits well with the opposition among the nobility, especially the non-Christians. They work constantly to undermine Wenceslaus.

Of a spiritual bent, he thinks of abdicating in favor of his younger brother, Boleslav, and going into a monastery, but reconsiders. He begins the building of the great Church of St. Vitus in Prague; in tribute to his grandmother he has her body brought from its grave in a Tetin church to be buried in the Church of St. George, built by his father. Despite frequent and sometimes violent opposition to Christianity, churches have continued to be erected in order to serve the steadily increasing number of faithful.

Trying to rule with both justice and mercy, guided by the principles his grandmother taught him, Wenceslaus recalls Drahomira to the court—her days of intrigue over. She has no part in the ensuing conspiracy, but Wenceslaus's brother does. In 929, having allied himself with the opposition when he believes his chance of succession to the throne is all but over (for a son is born to Wenceslaus), Boleslav, with three other men, intercepts Wenceslaus as he makes his way to Mass through a private passage from the castle. Just the evening before, Boleslav had invited him to a feast, and Wenceslaus now stops to thank his brother for the hospitality shown. Boleslav replies, "Yesterday I did my best to serve you fittingly, but this must be my service to-day." And he comes at Wenceslaus with a sword.

As Wenceslaus lies dying at the church door, he says to Boleslav, "Brother, may God forgive you."[1]

Like Ludmila, Wenceslaus, too, was immediately proclaimed a martyr. But Boleslav, having seized power, drove out the priests and persecuted Christians. His own mother and sister fled for safety, not knowing what he might do next. Eventually Otto the Great of Germany took steps forcing Boleslav to restore the faith, and the latter even accepted baptism before his death. His son, called Boleslav the Good, inspired by the memory of a saintly grandmother and uncle, succeeded in making all of Bohemia Christian.

Conversions were especially important to the church during this period because declining numbers resulted from chaotic conditions everywhere. The eastern Mediterranean lands and North Africa, containing much of the wealth of the church in terms of people, material goods and treasured shrines, had been lost to Islam in the two preceding centuries.

In an age when there was little for the church to cheer about (no pope emerged to give inspired leadership and even saints of note were rare), Ludmila's role as holy woman and promoter of Christianity became all the more valuable. She deservedly gets credit for a significant contribution in spreading the civilizing light of faith, extending its boundaries east.

The twentieth century added a footnote to her story: During the "Prague Spring" in 1968, the city's Wenceslaus Square (containing statues of both Wenceslaus and Ludmila) served as rallying point for the country's unsuccessful but courageous uprising against Communist rule. The longing for freedom could not be crushed, however. In 1989 the people of Prague gathered once more at the Square, this time accomplishing their goal in a remarkable "Velvet Revolution." Wenceslaus and Ludmila continue to be venerated and emulated by their people.

SWEET JESUS,

IT WAS A PAGAN CULTURE
THAT SURROUNDED LUDMILA.
EMBRACING CHRISTIANITY,
SHE MADE ENEMIES,
AND PAID THE PRICE.

WHILE OURS IS HARDLY A PAGAN CULTURE
(THOUGH SOME MIGHT ARGUE THAT),

I pray to stand strong in my faith
When morals are mocked.
Amen.

THE TENTH CENTURY

Adelaide, Empress of the Holy Roman Empire

Background

As the tenth century dawned, the great population shifts on the European continent were finally coming to an end. One indication of this was that a group of Danish Vikings put down roots half a century earlier on the Irish coast. Their settlement developed into Dublin.

In 911 another settlement of significance took place on the northwest coast of France when the French king bribed a tribe of Vikings with the offer of territory. He managed to convince the Norsemen (hence Normandy) that a steady income from commerce would profit them more in the long run than piracy.

The combination of invasions and migrations had been a severe hindrance to Europe's progress. Christianity had been hit especially hard by the destruction of monastic culture when

Vikings plundered and burned monasteries—not to mention the losses to Islam.

Recovery was in store, however. Just a year prior to the Normandy settlement, an even greater harbinger of happier times occurred in eastern France, in the region of Burgundy: the founding of a monastery called Cluny. It would be a name forever identified with church reform and spiritual revival.

In their darkest ages Europeans had been helpless. No strong leader had emerged after Charlemagne's death. There was a vacuum in the church, too, for no pope of moral stature or political clout had materialized either. In 936 that changed with the ascension to the German throne of Otto I, destined to become Otto the Great.

PAVIA, NORTHERN ITALY, CHRISTMAS DAY, 951

Otto I, king of Germany, marries Adelaide, twenty-year-old widow of the king of Lombardy. The wedding marks a happy ending to some trying and even frightening times for the young queen.

Her first husband was poisoned during a political struggle over control of Lombardy (northern Italy). Berengar, the man responsible for the poisoning, then tried to force Adelaide to marry his son. When she refused, Berengar imprisoned her in a castle near Lake Garda where, over a four-month period, she endured rough treatment.

Adelaide had loyal friends, however, and one of them, a priest named Martin, rescued her by digging a subterranean passage through which she made her escape. Hiding in the woods, they survived on fish from the lake until asylum could be arranged at a castle on church property.

As all this was going on, Otto, the powerful German king, marched south to straighten out the troubles in Lombardy, a move which promised to strengthen his own position. Once in

Italy, he met Adelaide (described as "a marvel of grace and beauty" by her biographer, Odilo, abbot of Cluny, who knew her personally). Otto surely made an impression too, for he was a giant of a man with a ruddy complexion and long red beard.

On his part, their marriage is politically wise, for Adelaide still bears a claim to the throne of Lombardy. Moreover, she is the daughter of the late Rudolf II of Burgundy, a small but strategically located kingdom in eastern France, and her mother comes from Swabia in southern Germany. But beyond that—and despite an almost twenty-year difference in age—the two fall in love.

Upon their return to Germany, Adelaide wins the affection of its people just as she had the Lombards'. In every important undertaking of government, she can be found at Otto's side; in a rare action, he has her image stamped on the reverse half of German coins.

He dreams of restoring the old Roman Empire to its former grandeur, making it God's kingdom on earth. But for all the politicking involved in that, Otto is a man of exemplary moral behavior. Those who work with the king dub him Otto the Pious.

Adelaide perceives as her special province bringing her influence to bear in matters of culture and religion. (The two are customarily intertwined.) On the cultural side, she and the ladies of the court create an atmosphere of learning through their encouragement and support of literature and the fine arts. Germany is just becoming the most prosperous country in Europe, and times are right for the high level of artistic achievement that history terms the Ottonian Renaissance.

Craftsmen produce exquisite work in gold filigree and ivory. One ivory book cover, for example, depicts in detail the celebration of the Mass. Convents enjoy a reputation as literary centers. At the convent of Gandersheim in Saxony, a nun named Hroswitha writes plays in classic Latin that are comparable in style to the Roman playwright Terence's, though much different in content. (Hroswitha's writings are being rediscovered by today's literary world.) Royal support also goes to monastic schools that are more like colleges and boast well-stocked libraries.

Adelaide knows how to promote spiritual enterprises, too. She presents abbots at court, and through her intercession many monasteries are founded or expanded. In fact, her generosity toward churches and monasteries is thought to be excessive, although no one voices a criticism aloud while Otto is alive.

Both Adelaide and Otto take particular interest in sending missionaries to the Slavic people who border Germany on the northeast, aiming to draw them into the rest of Christendom. Until that happens, the Slavs will constitute a threat. Another threat—this one to all of Europe—are the Magyars. When Otto defeats them in a brilliant victory in 955, he earns the title "the Great." He compels the roving warriors to settle in the territory later known as Hungary.

In 962 he and Adelaide journey to Rome to be crowned by the pope as emperor and empress. (Theirs was to be known as the Holy Roman Empire, though actually the term did not come into use until the twelfth century, when historians credited Otto with its founding.) Adelaide's old enemy Berengar is again stirring up trouble, this time in league with the pope. Otto had given the man a second chance during the Lombardy business, but further intrigues he will not allow. During subsequent imprisonment in Germany, Berengar dies and Adelaide takes in his young daughter, educating her to become one of the ladies at court. (Of Adelaide's own daughters one of them, Emma, from her first husband, marries the king of France; two of the three daughters she and Otto have profess as nuns.)

At the age of forty-two Adelaide becomes a widow for the second time when Otto dies while attending vespers at the Cathedral

of Magdeburg. Prior to that he had arranged, with the cooperation of the Byzantine Emperor, for marriage between his son Otto
and a Greek princess. Succeeding his father in 973, the nineteen-
year-old Otto II appears at first to be a ruler in the same mold, but
soon makes a move toward independence from the past. His wife
Theophano supports him and finds allies among the courtiers
who had objected privately in the past to Adelaide's generosity to
the church. When the situation threatens to turn into open conflict, the peace-loving Adelaide departs Germany, going to stay
with her brother Conrad at his court in Burgundy.

Nothing could be more natural than that she take an interest
now in conditions of the French church. In addition to giving aid
to abbeys, she sees to the rebuilding of the Monastery of St.
Martin of Tours, which had been destroyed by fire. (Its shrine in
honor of the saint is high on the list of Europe's important places
of pilgrimage.)

Church rebuilding of another sort is going on in the countryside of her native Burgundy where, early in the century, the
monastery at Cluny had been founded. Because of its abbots'
holiness, it becomes the center of a movement for ecclesiastical
reform—badly needed in the church but not forthcoming from
Rome. The papacy in the tenth century has sunk to its lowest
point in all of history; spiritual direction from that quarter is nonexistent. The Lateran Palace is better known for its orgies, and
control of the daily papal business is in the hands of leading
Roman families whose morals are absolutely appalling. Otto the
Great had worked to correct the pontifical mess through political
means. Cluny, on its part, starts with the reform of monasteries,
calling them back to New Testament values and practices. The
movement grows to encompass the whole of Christendom.

In her association with Cluny, Adelaide tells the abbot,
Mayeul, about the breach between her and her son Otto. She has

prayed long and offered numerous sacrifices in hope of reconciliation. When she appeals to Mayeul to mediate, he manages so successfully that a repentant Otto recalls his mother to court.

In thanksgiving, she sends a messenger loaded with gifts to the shrine at Tours. Among the gifts is Otto's finest cloak, accompanied by a prayer to Saint Martin. In it she recalls that the saint had once divided his cloak to cover a naked beggar. Later, a dream revealed that this was the Lord. (In the story of Saint Martin's life, the cloak represents heroic charity.) Adelaide invariably signed her letters: "Servant of the servants of God, sinner by nature, empress by the grace of God."[1]

On Adelaide's return to court Otto shows a willingness to listen to his mother's advice on reforms needed in government. On one occasion, when she expresses the wish that Mayeul be named pope (the incumbent has been murdered), Otto offers the abbot the papacy, but Mayeul says he's not interested. (The Holy Roman Emperor's approval is part of the selection process.)

In 982, while fighting the Saracens (as Arab Muslims were then called) in southern Italy, Otto suffers a disastrous defeat. The following year he appoints his mother viceroy of Lombardy. (It is common for the German monarch to name women to leading positions in government.) That same year he again heads for southern Italy, planning this time to seek a win against the Saracens. Stopping in Rome to plan the campaign, Otto contracts a fatal case of malaria.

His premature death while still in his twenties brings on a crisis for the empire. On the northern and eastern borders, enemies from without threaten. Within, a violent struggle erupts over the question of who will assume the regency, since Otto III is just three years old.

Although Adelaide and her daughter-in-law Theophano both qualify as legitimate rulers, the two are so different in nature and outlook that joint rule seems impossible. To ensure the peace, Adelaide returns to her position in Pavia as viceroy of Lombardy. The Lombards revere their former queen and, with this in her favor, she succeeds in keeping the strategic territory loyal to the empire.

Theophano cannot bear to see her mother-in-law prospering. During the next few years, Theophano continually tries to undercut Adelaide's high standing. In 991 Theophano makes the curious remark that if she lives another full year, she will manage to oust Adelaide as viceroy. But before year's end, while on a trip through western Germany, Theophano unexpectedly dies.

This time there is no question that Adelaide will take over as regent of the empire until her grandson comes of age in 995. For guidance, she relies on Willigis, Archbishop of Mainz, who helped end the crisis when Otto II died, and on her spiritual director, Odilo, a young monk at Cluny destined soon to be its abbot. Adelaide typically shows no ill will toward those courtiers who earlier had sided with Theophano.

When Otto III reaches his majority, the sixty-four-year-old empress gladly retires from administering the vast empire. In her new freedom, Adelaide can devote full time to prayer and the foundation and restoration of houses for monks and nuns.

Still engaged in peacemaking, too, she is en route to Burgundy in December 999 to effect a reconciliation between her nephew, the king, and his rebellious subjects when she falls ill and stops at Selz, a monastery on the Rhine that she had founded. With Adelaide at the end is Odilo, now abbot of Cluny, who observes in her biography that despite her lofty position as empress, Adelaide never forgot that there is only one Lord. But perhaps the most telling assessment of her character is the remark often made of her that "she never forgot a kindness, nor ever remembered an injury."

AFTERWARD

From the middle of the tenth century to the start of the eleventh, Germany took the lead in Europe, both politically and artistically. For the fresh surge of creativity known as the Ottonian Renaissance, historians credit the imperial court where Adelaide presided over matters of culture as well as religion. The artistic achievements of this renaissance set the tone for art all through the Middle Ages.

In her close association with both the aesthetic realm and spiritual reform, Adelaide played a critical role in shaping the Christian culture of Western Europe. Her friend Odilo of Cluny, by the way, is considered the greatest among all its great abbots of this period. One guesses he shared Adelaide's love of peace, for Cluny took the lead in attempting to restrict the incessant warfare among feudal lords that caught peasants in the middle with predictable devastation. An idea surfacing in 990 eventually resulted in the "Truce of God," whereby fighting was suspended every Friday, Saturday and Sunday. Later Lent was added to the "closed season."

Missionaries who had been sent to convert the Slavs living on Germany's northeastern border (the area comprising Poland) were overwhelmingly successful. In the eleventh century Poland could be called thoroughly Christian.

In 999 Adelaide's grandson Otto III had his former tutor, a scholarly and devout man, named pope. Sylvester II's papacy would herald a revival of the Christian spirit where it was most urgently needed—in the papacy itself. In the following century new laws for selecting a pope would begin the process of eliminating outside interference.

Adelaide's death came just two weeks before the start of the year 1000. The approach of the millennium brought with it a pervasive mood of fear among the common people that the end of the world was in sight. When the date passed without the earth disintegrating in a vast conflagration, the universal sigh of relief was followed by a burst of energy and enthusiasm in all things religious and secular.

PRINCE OF PEACE,

EVER THE PEACEMAKER,
EVEN AT THE LAST,
ADELAIDE JOURNEYED ONCE MORE
TO HEAL THE WOUNDS
OF DISCORD.

BLESSED THE PEACEMAKERS,
TOO OFTEN REVILED.
GIVE ME THE COURAGE
TO JOIN THEIR RANKS.
AMEN.

10 : ADELAIDE, EMPRESS OF THE HOLY ROMAN EMPIRE

THE ELEVENTH CENTURY

MARGARET OF SCOTLAND

BACKGROUND

After the Magyars were defeated by Otto the Great and forced to stay put in the Hungarian plains, they turned their once-ferocious energy into more constructive channels. Mingling with the Slavic people who had earlier settled in Hungary, they went to work to develop the fertile land as well as its gold and silver mines. Conversions to Christianity began late in the tenth century. In 997 Stephen, whose father was the country's first ruler to be baptized, became head of government. Known for his piety and special care for the poor (he would later be canonized), Stephen worked with Pope Sylvester II (former tutor of Otto III) to set up an organized hierarchy so that the church could firmly establish itself.

During his reign (997–1038) Stephen gave refuge to a member of the English royal family. A force of Danes had invaded England. The country's king, Edmund Ironside, was compelled in 1016 to share power with one of the invaders. Edmund died that same year. His son Edward, just an infant, was taken out of the country, and that saved his life. Welcome was found at the court of Hungary, far enough from England for him to avoid being victimized by the Danish usurper. (Nothing is known of the mother's fate.) Edward stayed in Hungary, where he grew up, married and had three children.

Back in England in the same year that Edward's daughter Margaret was born, his uncle, now King Edward the Confessor, was forced to enter into an arranged marriage with the daughter of his greatest political adversary. Edward was revered for his personal sanctity whence the title of "Confessor"—but lacked the toughness to govern effectively in a turbulent age. As time passed with no heir (it's said the marriage was never consummated), the question of succession became a matter of concern to all parties connected with the throne.

DUNFERMLINE, SCOTLAND, OCTOBER 1068

Departing London by ship, twenty-three-year-old Princess Margaret, her mother, younger brother and sister survive the voyage through a stormy North Sea. Once their coasting vessel heads inland along an estuary known as the Firth of Forth, the weather improves and the scenery too, for this is Scotland's golden autumn.

At his fortress-palace on a crag high above the firth, Malcolm Canmore, the king, gets word that the alien ship that has dropped anchor in the bay carries political refugees from England. He hurries to welcome them.

Margaret's family had deemed it wise to seek asylum in the nearest country. For the young Anglo-Saxon princess, being a political exile is hardly a novel experience. Until she was about twelve, she had lived at the court of Hungary, since her father, though in the line of succession to the English throne, had not felt it safe to go back to England. (Margaret's mother was a German princess related to the Hungarian royal family.) After Margaret's father received an invitation to return and was advised that he need no longer fear danger, he and the family journeyed to England. But he died almost immediately upon their arrival.

With close kin Edward the Confessor on the throne, the family elected to stay on. The English court was a friendly place to be—until the childless Edward succumbed to an illness in January, 1066. In a contest for the throne, the outcome of the Battle of Hastings determined the winner, and the Duke of Normandy was crowned king on Christmas Day, 1066. (History knows it as the Norman Conquest.) Not surprisingly, any potential rival would be viewed with suspicion.

Had Margaret's brother Edgar been of hardier character, he might have attempted to recover the throne. As his father's heir, he did have a legitimate claim. Instead, the decision was made to look elsewhere for a home, bringing the family to Scotland and the court of Malcolm Canmore.

Malcolm himself had experienced exile as a boy. When his father was murdered in 1040 by Macbeth, he sought the protection of the English king for more than a dozen years, leaving when he was of an age to fight to reclaim the Scottish throne— close to the time that Margaret's family first arrived in England.

When Margaret and Malcolm meet, the king is in his late thirties, a widower with a son, and more than a little attracted to the young princess seeking his protection. As the *Anglo-Saxon Chronicle* puts it: "Then King Malcolm began to yearn for Edgar's sister as his wife."[1]

Margaret's inclination has long been toward the contemplative life. Her sister Christina will later become abbess of an English monastery, which her mother will also join. Whatever the reason, however—perhaps to make life more secure for her family—Margaret finally gives in to the persistence of Malcolm who, though known for his tempestuous nature, never exhibits it with her. He can guess what marriage to her will be like, for her very first act as queen is to build a large church.

Next she addresses herself to the rather rustic ways of the court. The gently bred but strong-willed Margaret determines to soften the rough manners of the knights attached to service at the palace (though it is less palatial in appearance than fortress-like). Distressed that the men leave the table the moment they finish eating, she wants them at least to take time to say grace, a prayer of thanksgiving for the meal.

Rather than hurt their feelings with a lecture, she starts her crusade by arranging that the knights who follow her wishes will be offered a special cup of wine—the Grace Cup—sent to the table by her. Soon all the knights can be seen praying after mealtime. (For many years, the Grace Cup, or St. Margaret's Blessing as it was also called, was a feature of every Scottish festival.)

Nor does the queen neglect the ladies at court. She organizes them to study Scripture together and teaches them the *Opus Angelicum*, "Angel's Work," setting up in one of the great rooms of the castle a workshop for liturgical art. There the ladies make priestly vestments, altar linens and tapestries for church decoration.

Organizer that she is, Margaret has her own regime of work, study and prayer. Brought up under the influence of Benedictine ideas, she asks a Lincolnshire Benedictine monk named Turgot to be her chaplain. The biography he later writes supplies many of the personal details known about Margaret. Little is known, however, of the queen's physical appearance, except that she is tall.

The beauty of her nature seems to count for more to the chroni-clers. There must have been a radiance about her to which Malcolm duly responded, for it is said that "her loving spirit set his on fire."[2]

Though unable to read or write, Malcolm, seeing the pleasure she derives from books, takes note of those she particularly likes, and then has craftsmen embellish them with gold and precious gems. Such are his feelings for Margaret, "he would turn over and examine books which she used either for her devotions or her study; and whenever he heard her say that she was fonder of one of them than the others, this one he too used to look at with spe-cial affection, kissing it, and often taking it in his hands."[3] (Her most treasured book, her illuminated Gospel Book—though long since minus the richly ornamented cover—is preserved today in the Bodleian Library at Oxford University.)

Books represent Margaret's one personal extravagance. She is otherwise lavish only in the way she spends herself—and the royal treasury—in unflagging service to others, the poor foremost among them. (To insure that the poor have at least one day of rest, she insists on observance of the Sabbath.) Margaret takes seriously the words of her favorite books, the Gospels, and sees Christ in every person in need. She does more than go out to visit the poor and sick. Daily the court chamberlain is detailed to bring in six of the poorest people. Before feeding them, the queen washes their feet in the humble act of a slave. When Malcolm is at home, she persuades him to join her.

During the seasons of Lent and Advent, the royal hall is trans-formed into a great dining space for several hundred of the poor, who are provided the same kind of food and drink as the court enjoys. The queen helps serve down one side of the hall, the king on the other.

Throughout the year all her life Margaret regularly supports two dozen of the poor out of the state treasury. When that runs dry, she helps herself to her husband's personal funds. (Margaret's biographer wrote that "this pious plundering the king always took pleasantly and in good part."[4]) She also convinces Malcolm to fund the almshouses and hospitals that she establishes.

Justice concerns her too. She insists that her husband do something to curb the soldiers' pillaging their own countrymen as well as to restrain the nobles from feuding among themselves. The violence must stop, she says, and he agrees, for Scotland has trouble enough just defending itself against that rich and powerful neighbor to the south.

Margaret is not above sending her own spies about the country to determine who among the Scots are mistreating captives taken in the skirmishes with England. If the situation warrants, she will pay the ransom required to set a captive free.

The church of Scotland comes in for scrutiny too. It disturbs her that liturgical practices have crept in that differ from the rest of the Western church, for she understands the tremendous unifying strength of a universal liturgy with the symbolic value of uniformity from one end of Europe to the other. As to people failing to receive the Eucharist, holding the sacrament in such awe that they feel too unworthy, she exclaims: "What!... Shall no one that is a sinner taste that holy mystery? If so, then it follows that no one at all should receive it, for no one is pure from sin."[5] Citing the Gospel as well as commentaries by church fathers to convince the faithful of the graces available, she induces many to return to a reception of the Eucharist not only at Easter but on other feasts too.

Above all, the queen worries about the lukewarmness of the hierarchy and clergy toward their religion. She summons church leaders to a synod—first to hear their point of view, then to explain her feelings, based on Scripture and other authoritative writings.

Prior to the synod, there had not been gatherings to discuss countrywide church policy. Now other councils follow as Margaret attempts to correct abuses, promote better education for the clergy and advance spirituality. An account of one council session tells of Malcolm's presence to provide backing for anything Margaret may choose to do. But she is in charge and leads the discussion. According to her biographer, the proud and able warrior is ready to bend to his wife's will because he sees in her "the incarnation of all that was pure and holy."[6]

She is also the mother of their eight children. With all her other responsibilities, Margaret finds time to instruct them personally in their faith and to supervise their studies. To accomplish so much, Margaret has learned to do with little sleep.

At an indeterminate time the royal family moves its residence across the Firth of Forth to Edinburgh on the south shore, where Margaret spends many happy hours with her children in the castle garden. In Edinburgh today her oratory on Castle Rock has the distinction of being the city's oldest building. (The name Edinburgh comes from Edwin, king of Northumbria. After conquering the district in the seventh century, he built a fortress called Edwin's Burgh. Edwin, you may remember, was the great-uncle of Hilda of Whitby.)

The one cloud that darkens Margaret's life is the brutality of warfare common to her time. On this she and Malcolm, otherwise so close in spirit, do not agree. Where she sees inhumanity, he sees necessity. When his country's independence is at stake, no amount of eloquence on Margaret's part holds sway.

Periodic invasions by England are countered with raids into English territory by Malcolm's troops. (Some of the raids, it deserves noting, are on behalf of Margaret's brother Edgar, whose penchant for political intriguing gets him into trouble. He regularly runs to Malcolm for help.)

As penance for the violence, Margaret fasts to extremes despite her confessor Turgot's advice to the contrary. He warns that her health will suffer.

A treaty between the two countries brings a temporary peace, but in 1093 promises are broken and Malcolm must go off to war again. He takes his two oldest sons with him. As her health begins to fail rapidly and with a premonition that Malcolm's expedition will end in his death, Margaret summons Turgot, who had left the court two years before to become prior at Durham.

"There are two things which I beg of you," Margaret says to Turgot. "One is that as long as you survive, you will remember me in your prayers; the other is, that you will take some care about my sons and daughters. Lavish your affection upon them; teach them before all things to love and fear God; never cease instructing them."[7] Turgot promises to abide by her wishes.

Margaret's worst fears are realized. Not only is Malcolm killed, but their eldest son, too. After hearing the news, she dies within a matter of days. Margaret and Malcolm are both buried at Dunfermline Abbey, which the two had founded in the early years of their marriage.

AFTERWARD

Near Dunfermline is a stone called St. Margaret's Stone. Here, says tradition, the queen used to sit so that anyone in trouble might come to her. While this may not be literally true, it is likely founded on the fact that the public—including beggars—had easy access to her.

Acting always with exquisite courtesy toward each person, rich or poor, Margaret practiced the rare art of bringing about reform without ruffling feathers. In her reforms she led Scotland out of its previous isolation and into line with the rest of Western

Christendom. A sense of a common community was developing throughout Europe. With Margaret began her country's integration into the cultural and religious society of Europe. Solidifying ties in the church of the West meant all the more since, in 1054, the final break had come between Rome and the Orthodox church of the East.

Margaret's sons, serving in turn as kings, carried on her policies, which inaugurated a golden age for Scotland that was to last two hundred years.

GRACIOUS GOD,

IT'S BECAUSE MARGARET SAW CHRIST
IN EVERY PERSON SHE MET,
THAT THIS WOMAN OF GRACE
COULD LAVISH LOVE UNFETTERED
ON THE POOREST OF THE POOR.

DO I SEE CHRIST SO EASILY?
OR AM I BLIND TO HIS PRESENCE
IN THE LEAST LIKELY, LEAST LOVABLE?
I NEED TO TAKE THE BLINDERS OFF.
AMEN.

THE TWELFTH CENTURY

HILDEGARD OF BINGEN

BACKGROUND

Christendom stretched from Scotland to the borders of Russia where in 957 Olga, duchess of Kiev, had become one of the first Russian converts. The sense of a kingdom crossing political boundaries was based on mutual sharing of Christian culture and values.

The eleventh century had seen the papacy grow increasingly influential under a succession of strong popes capable of enforcing their decrees. In 1075, for instance, celibacy, which had long been an issue, became the norm when Pope Gregory VII insisted on it. Popes also took over calling church councils. In the past these had been held in the East, often at the behest of the emperor there. Since the final split between the church of the East and the West in 1054, popes saw that councils met in the West and presided over them.

The spiritual vigor of Western Christendom could be viewed in the construction of cathedrals such as Notre Dame and a mounting veneration for the Virgin Mary (though women religious must now look to male authority for the last word). Other signs of new life were the founding of several reform-minded orders of monks. The Carthusians (1084) and Cistercians (1098) both aimed at combating laxities creeping in as the Cluniac movement lost its edge and became history. Some individuals called for a return to the simplicity of the Apostolic Age, accusing both papacy and clerics of spending too much time on temporal affairs, but their voices were muted—most often by ecclesiastical force.

The foregoing trends seemed to coalesce when Pope Urban II convened the Council of Clermont (France) in 1095 and issued his famous call for a Crusade to rescue the Holy Land from the infidel Turks. The response was immediate and enthusiastic. Such was the pope's authority as well as the fervor of the times. The great stain on that first Crusade came as the knights of Christendom, in their march eastward across the continent, stopped long enough to massacre European Jews by the tens of thousands.

Trier, Germany, Winter of 1147-1148

Pope Eugenius III calls a synod during which the participants discuss the visions of a talked-about Rhineland nun, Hildegard of Bingen. A commission headed by the bishop of Verdun returns from its investigation of the nun to report: "I found her, Holy Father...as a flaming torch which our Lord has lighted in His Church." To which the pope replies, "Then we must not put it under a bushel."[1]

He writes to Hildegard, letting her know that the synod has concluded her visions come from God, compliments her on being so favored but also cautions her against pride. In a letter of response Hildegard thanks the pope, then, referring to current abuses in the church, tells Eugenius he must work harder to correct them.

Despite the sound of it, Hildegard never finds her role as reformer an easy one. As late as her seventies, when she is famous throughout Christendom for her gift of prophecy, she confides to the monk Guibert, later one of her biographers: "For my part I am always in fear and trembling because I have not any security as to what I am able to do." Only God's support sustains her, she explains, "as on wings whose flight is beyond comprehension and which soar in the heavens in spite of all contrary winds."[2]

Had she followed her own inclinations, Hildegard might easily have remained in obscurity all of her life. Born in 1098 in the village of Bermersheim bei Alzey, southwest of Mainz, in Germany's Rhineland region, Hildegard has been described as a "solitary and unusual child" who, at the age of eight, became her parents' "tithe to the Lord"—a not-uncommon practice then (but more common when the youngster was "different"). Her father, a member of the nobility, though untitled, and a knight in the service of the local duke, placed his tenth child in the care of the duke's daughter Jutta. This holy and learned woman, twenty years old at the time of her vows, had chosen to live in a two-room cell adjoining the church of a Benedictine monastery in the neighborhood. The only other companion at Disibodenberg was to be one of Jutta's poor cousins, there to aid with domestic chores.

A window provided access for the passing through of food and other necessities. It was also the means by which visitors seeking counsel from the holy Jutta could speak with her at designated times. Her reputation for sanctity also drew more aspirants to the enclosed life.

Around the age of fourteen, Hildegard took vows as a nun. Quiet years of prayer, work and study followed. When Jutta died in 1136, Hildegard, at age thirty-eight, was appointed superior, though much against her will, for the limelight was never what she sought. Jutta's original community had grown to about a dozen women living according to the Benedictine Rule. Although still located at Disibodenberg, they by then enjoyed a convent of their own.

Hildegard's health, never the best even in childhood, was afflicted still more by the interior struggles brought on by having to face exterior ordeals. Since at least the age of five, she experienced visions, seen not in a physical sense but with spiritual sight in the depths of her soul, gifting her with revelations and prophecies. The visions took their toll. So powerfully was her entire self claimed by communion with God, at times Hildegard thought she would break. To Bernard, the renowned abbot of Clairvaux, motherhouse of the reform-minded Cistercian Order, she once confessed that the visions burned her soul. As she explained to him in a letter: "Wretched, and indeed more than wretched in my womanly condition, I have from earliest childhood seen great marvels which my tongue has power to express but which the Spirit of God has taught me that I may believe. Steadfast and gentle father, in your kindness respond to me, your unworthy servant who has never, from her earliest childhood, lived one hour free from anxiety."[3] (Of all the great figures of the twelfth century, which Hildegard's life nearly spans, Bernard alone seems to have escaped a critical review by her. He was the most influential man of that era.)

Though often confined to bed for weeks at a time—and even when well, having difficulty walking—she continued her single-handed campaign to redirect the many worldly minds in the hierarchy and clergy to spiritual concerns. For any individual to embark on such a course takes rare courage. For a woman of her day, it was a double burden, and Hildegard knew it.

The seemingly uneventful years that preceded her entrance onto the world stage were marked by mystical experience. Shy and sensitive by nature, she was scarcely ready to share her spiritual side with others, fearing that people were bound to laugh at her. Finally Hildegard told her confessor, who advised her to write down her visions and revelations.

The nun resisted until, as she explained, "I heard a voice from heaven which said to me, 'Relate these marvels; write down the things which thou hast learnt and say, In the year 1141 of the Incarnation of the Son of God, at the age of 42 years, 7 months, a fiery light of wondrous brightness coming from the open heavens, dispersed itself all about my Brain and all about my heart and all about my Breast as a flame; yet not such as burns, but such as warms.'"[4] And then she describes being illuminated with understanding of many books, including the Old and New Testaments.

This prompted her to begin writing her first and most celebrated book, *Scito Vias Domini* ("Know the Ways of the Lord"), often referred to by its abbreviated title, *Scivias*. The work took almost ten years to complete. Meanwhile, the woman destined to tackle major problems in church and society found herself doing battle first with the abbot of Disibodenberg.

Her community has grown to more than fifty women and present convent quarters prove too cramped. Because the monks of Disibodenberg's need for more space has already made a big dent in what is available, Hildegard decides on a move to Rupertsberg, a site much closer to Bingen.

Technically the nuns owe obedience to the abbot, and he strongly opposes the idea. The thought of losing Hildegard along with her newfound prestige (and the income that might result) upsets his plans. As habitually happens, Hildegard's health soon suffers (which some modern studies of Hildegard refer to as "passive resistance")—until, in a vision, God commands the move. Her earliest biography explains it this way: "And she suffered this kind of illness...whenever she delayed or doubted to perform the business of the heavenly will through womanly fear" (*Vita*, Bk. 1).[5] The pope subsequently gives his approval for a new convent.

Reassured, Hildegard recovers sufficiently to oversee the construction at Rupertsberg, including one innovative feature: plumbing that pipes water for use inside the building. (Like all authentic mystics, she knows when it is time to come back down to earth.)

As a way of forestalling future problems with the abbot, she initiates the lengthy process of putting Rupertsberg under the protection of the archbishop at Mainz, and eventually the request is granted.

The move to the new convent takes place in 1150, and the community begins to flourish as never before. These nuns are a talented lot—women of considerable creativity in music and the arts. Under Hildegard's direction they illuminate manuscripts including, possibly, the magnificent ones in *Scivias* that depict the abbess's visions. (Another possibility is that the illustrations were produced by friends who were monks at an abbey in Trier, but still done under her supervision.)

Hildegard also composes dozens of hymns and writes the first known morality play, *Ordo Virtutum* ("The Ritual of the Virtues"). The play deals with the mystery of good and evil in life. Set to music, it has sometimes been compared to opera. (The play is still being performed, and recordings of her other musical compositions are available too.)

Other writings include commentaries on the Gospels, biographies of Saint Rupert and Saint Disibod, Celtic missionaries to the Rhineland in earlier centuries, several more books dealing with her visions, as well as books on natural history and medicines—one of these of encyclopedic proportions.

Hildegard's interest in the study of medicine stems from her own chronic experience with illness, and some of her theories come surprisingly close to later scientific discoveries, such as one on the circulation of blood. Her monastery garden blooms with medicinal herbs, which are not reserved for nuns only but available also to sick people from the surrounding area who show up at the infirmary in anticipation of the abbess's healing ways. She is said to have mastered the art of doctoring.

Many other visitors seeking advice on spiritual matters, princes of the church and humble pilgrims, too, appear on the doorstep. Then there are those the monastery makes room for as permanent residents—poor, older women—so that their later years might be comfortable, according to one biographer who lived for years in the neighborhood.

With her books and a voluminous correspondence Hildegard now requires the help of two secretaries to whom she dictates. One is her longtime friend, Volmar, a monk at Disibodenberg, who acts in this capacity until his death in 1173; the other is Richardis of Stade, a cousin of Jutta, and a favorite among her nuns.

Once the Rupertsberg community is well established, she feels free to go out on apostolic journeys to deliver her prophetic words in person. To preach in public requires ecclesiastical approval, usually restricted to the ordained. Hers is a rare privilege. In her fifties Hildegard takes to the road, traveling by horseback throughout Germany and into France. She does so into her seventies. Because the roads are not safe, an armed escort accompanies her.

Though on the surface the twelfth century appears to be a great one for Western Christendom, with the authority of the papacy firmly grounded, Hildegard looks deeper, sees all that is wrong and becomes convinced of the absolute necessity to speak out no matter what the personal cost. Not having sought the gift of prophecy, she admits to finding it a "painful job."

Wearing a black habit (she wears white only for the great feasts), the abbess makes a powerful impression as she ascends pulpits in both cathedrals and religious communities to attack the evils of corruption and a too-luxurious lifestyle among the clergy. She commends only those who prove themselves soldiers for Christ. Her preaching tours, incidentally, take her not only to churches and monasteries, but also to marketplaces and public squares—something unheard of for a woman.

Hildegard pictures the ailing church as a weeping mother in pain. In forceful language she accuses bishops and abbots of pre-ferring a sword to a shepherd's staff, letting their involvement in secular business—the administration of monastic lands, for example—take precedence over spiritual guidance of their flock. The laity, she admonishes church leaders, suffer as a result. Opposition there may be when her words prick consciences, but Hildegard also instills in some the courage to make changes, infusing her own ardor for greater commitment, and brings reas-surance to the faithful. Many hear "the voice of Christ" in her prophesying.

When clergy in Cologne request a copy of a speech, she sends with it a letter in which she tells of being "completely exhausted" from her round of speech-making. The nun indicates too an abil-ity to smile at herself, noting with wry amusement that though nothing but a shy, poor woman, she is in the absurd situation of lecturing "wise men" who hold degrees as masters of arts and doctors.

Hildegard offers an insightful look in comparing herself to Judith, the apocryphal woman of Hebrew Scriptures, who single-handedly slew the Assyrian general threatening to destroy Israel and thereby brought peace to her people. As the story of that victory goes: "...but the Lord Almighty has thwarted them by a woman's hand."

Whether by letter or direct encounter, Hildegard confronts the greatest leaders of her era: Henry II of England, remembered as the king responsible for the murder of Archbishop Thomas Becket; Henry's wife, Eleanor of Aquitaine; and German emperors, including Conrad III and the fearsome Frederick Barbarossa, who invites her to his palace.

The century was plagued by nearly a dozen antipopes as kings and emperors made futile attempts to regain control of the papacy. On one occasion, when Barbarossa decides to name an antipope, Hildegard fires off a letter denouncing his action as that of a "madman."

A fighter to the literal end, her last great battle with the power structure calls attention to an often overlooked spirit of compassion as well as her sense of justice. She runs into trouble with canons at Mainz Cathedral because of a situation that comes about when a young man is allowed burial in the Rupertsberg cemetery. Though he had been excommunicated by the archbishop (whom Hildegard had already reproved for living the good life in Italy instead of residing in the archdiocese), the abbess, whose love excluded no one, is of the firm belief that the man truly repented. Since he had received the last sacraments before his death, he must certainly have made his peace with God. What is more, a vision confirms her belief.

Nevertheless, ecclesiastical officials order her to remove the body from sacred ground. When she refuses, her convent is threatened with interdict: No Masses will be said, no sacraments given to her community, no liturgical music sung—and she loves her music. Even the church bells cannot be rung.

Eighty-year-old Hildegard goes out to the cemetery and with her walking staff erases the lines around the young man's grave so that his burial place cannot be detected. A furious archbishop gets the pope to agree to the interdict.

The impasse drags on for a year, causing Hildegard immense sorrow, but she remains resolute. Only after protracted negotiations and the intercession of influential friends is the ban withdrawn. Hildegard dies just a few months later in September 1179.

AFTERWARD

Certainly one of the major figures of her time, Hildegard left her mark on the twelfth century with an extraordinary range of achievements. Had she been only a mystic and writer of spiritual literature, or only a theologian and scientist, or only an artist and musician, or only a prophet and reformer, her life would have been remarkable enough. But she was all of the above!

The flavor of her prophesying, incidentally, may be found in passages on the fate of the wicked that have been compared to descriptions in Dante's *Inferno*, written about a hundred years later.

In overcoming the "handicap," as Hildegard saw it, of being a woman in a world controlled by man, she served as the conscience of the church. In her mysticism she led the way as the first of the great Rhineland mystics. She left a legacy of music as well as inspired writings. In some ways—her concern for the environment as exemplified by a creation-centered theology—Hildegard is almost more twenty-first century than twelfth. For what is more contemporary than her observation: "All nature is at the disposal of humankind. We are to work with it. Without it we cannot survive"?[6]

A reawakened interest in Hildegard in recent times began in

the 1950s, when her writings were translated from the Latin into German, making her work available to a wider audience. Though never officially canonized (due apparently to a snag in the bureaucratic process), in 1970 the Vatican's Sacred Congregation gave permission to Catholic dioceses in Germany to honor Hildegard with a feast day on September 17. Upon the eight hundredth anniversary of Hildegard's death, Pope John Paul II referred to her as "an outstanding saint," and "a light to her people and her time [who] shines out more brightly today."[7]

The daughter house Hildegard founded in 1165 at Eibingen, across the river from Rupertsberg (the latter was destroyed in a war long ago) keeps her memory alive. And scholars are eagerly delving into the *Life of Jutta* (written c. 1140), a manuscript discovered in 1991, valuing it as a source for new information about Hildegard's early years.

In assessing the remarkably wide-ranging life of Hildegard, what might best be remembered is her essential message: What the individual heart needs is to be flooded with love, and what the church needs is to be holy.

SPIRIT OF WISDOM,

IN THE FINAL CHAPTER OF HER LIFE,
HILDEGARD IS ONCE MORE SUSTAINED
BY HER BELIEF IN GOD'S WILL:
DOING WHAT'S RIGHT,
NO MATTER THE CONSEQUENCES.

HOW STRONG ARE MY CONVICTIONS?
HOW CAN I KNOW GOD'S WILL?
QUESTIONS THAT NEED ASKING,
QUESTIONS THAT NEED ANSWERING.
AMEN.

THE THIRTEENTH CENTURY

CLARE OF ASSISI

BACKGROUND

"Undiminished vitality" aptly describes the thirteenth century, which is also often called "the greatest of centuries" for Western Christendom. Never again would the papacy achieve quite such supremacy in both the sacred and secular realm. One of the greatest popes, Innocent III, was elected while still in his thirties and proved admirably effective as churchman and statesman as well. There was much to oversee since a considerable bureaucracy had by now been created to administer the manifold responsibilities of the church.

This took money. Peter's Pence was only a start. (It originated in the eighth century as an annual penny tax on households, hence the name.) Next, taxes were levied on churches around Christendom to help pay the bills.

There was money to be had, especially in Italy, for its towns prospered as a result of the East-West trade and travel (including pilgrimages) engendered by the Crusades. Venice, for example, served as the chief embarkation port for the Holy Land. But even in the comparatively small town of Assisi in the Umbrian Hills of central Italy, an ever-expanding merchant class was ready to challenge the power of local feudal lords. Though peasants still constituted the majority of the population in Europe, society was in transition.

Amid all the exuberance of the era, many of the laity viewed with dissatisfaction the sight of a church grown mighty in its wealth and consequent worldliness. It seemed to contradict the very gospel values it preached. A longing to see a return to the purity of authentic gospel living began to stir.

ASSISI, ITALY, MARCH 18, 1212

Eighteen-year-old Clare di Favarone slips away Palm Sunday night from her parents' home to meet a thirty-year-old preacher, Francis Bernardone, in the woods outside the town walls. She is accompanied by a trusted friend; he, by his band of Poor Brothers carrying burning torches. They enter the Chapel of St. Mary of the Angels and, before the altar, Clare renounces the world, consecrating herself to God. Francis cuts off her long golden hair; she lays aside the jewels she wears and exchanges her elegant gown for a garment of gray sackcloth.

Once this has been accomplished, however, a question arises: What will Francis do with her now? Her family's reaction is bound to be stormy. Her father, of the landed aristocracy, had planned marriage for his beautiful and intelligent daughter, though ever since Clare first heard Francis preach of Jesus' love and the joy of holy poverty, she has yearned to join his company. To that end, she had been meeting him secretly for the past year— always with a companion to chaperone her properly.

13 :: CLARE OF ASSISI

Until more permanent arrangements can be made, Francis places Clare in a nearby convent. Her family soon discovers that she has run off, apparently under the influence of that (some say crazy) son of the cloth merchant, whose recently organized company of friars beg for their daily bread. A contingent of male relatives shows up at the convent to bring the young woman home. They are scandalized to see her with shorn hair, barefoot and dressed like the poorest peasant. Clare absolutely refuses to let them take her back.

The nuns Francis talked into harboring Clare decide they do not need that kind of trouble, and he finds a second convent for her. Here one of Clare's younger sisters, fifteen-year-old Catherine (soon to take Agnes as her name in religion), joins her. (A sometimes monastic custom, a name change signified rebirth in religion.) The family, understandably upset that two of their daughters are now in the hands of the wandering preacher, create an even bigger disturbance. Again they fail. These nuns also want no more of such goings-on. Clare herself is happy about leaving, for she has been at this convent just long enough to observe the nuns wrangling with the bishop over the community's commercial farming enterprise. She has different ideas about religious life for women.

Francis, having obtained permission from Benedictines who own the property, next takes the two young women to a little house beside the Church of San Damiano. This was the church he had rebuilt after hearing the voice of the Lord say, "Francis, go and repair my house, which is falling completely into ruin."[1] Taking the instruction literally—just as he does with gospel teachings—he had done his best to mend the tumbledown building. (Incidentally, it was common for small churches to have above the doorway the words *Domus mea*, "My house.") San Damiano remains close to Francis' heart, therefore making it special to Clare.

The accommodations at San Damiano are a far cry from what Favarone's daughters are accustomed to. Despite the austere surroundings, they are soon joined by other young friends and kinswomen from the noble families of Assisi who find Francis' message irresistible, for he practices what he preaches (penance, poverty and joy).

Perhaps Clare dreamed fleetingly of walking in his footsteps in the same manner as the dozen or so members of the brotherhood. But even the idealistic Francis recognizes the impossibility of a woman—let alone a high-born one—tromping about Italy, begging for her daily bread. No, convent life in some form is the only practical solution.

But, as Clare will insist to her dying breath, it must be a life of absolute poverty—even though the church itself has difficulty with the idea. By now, ecclesiastical holdings constitute more than half the lands of Europe. In religious orders members may vow poverty in the sense of retaining no possessions as individuals, yet they hold collective ownership of income-producing property such as agricultural land. This property, often given as an endowment to a convent or monastery, ensures its financial stability. But Clare and her Poor Ladies aim to hold only enough land to maintain the privacy of their monastery and to cultivate only enough garden to supply the needs of the sisters' table.

All her life Clare will be ready to stand up to those who in theory have power over her, but when Francis says she is to live an enclosed existence of some sort, she accepts it, as long as that life adheres faithfully to the gospel. The two are twin souls, finding their security in Providence rather than possessions.

The time is right for a venture such as theirs, for the thirteenth century is a spirited age. The people of Western Christendom build soaring cathedrals, engage in feudal wars, go on Crusades or aspire to join the growing class of merchants and artisans. The majority of the population still belongs to the peasantry, and there exists a great gap between them and church officials, who often seem to prefer high living to high ideals. The general mood among the more pious-minded laity becomes one of disenchantment with the institutional church. Out of this has sprung popular religious movements of varying types. One such are the Beguines, communities of laywomen free from ecclesiastical governance, and engaged in work to support themselves, prayer and service to the sick and needy. They take no vows. Francis' own little company begins as a lay movement, though he humbly agrees to ordination as a deacon in order to preach the gospel.

This then is the state of affairs when Pope Innocent III takes time from a heavy schedule to hear the petition of a group which has come to Rome seeking approval of a new order to be known as the Friars Minor. Their leader appears insignificant enough, but the pope senses something about the man. In another few years, around 1215, Innocent will find himself also approving the Rule of an associated group, the Poor Ladies. Clare asks the pope to grant them the privilege of possessing nothing; in agreeing, he observes with wonder that such a privilege has never been asked of Rome before.

In its first years, before papal sanction, San Damiano operates rather informally, coming under Francis' personal direction. He provides the women with a very simple rule of life that emphasizes, as Clare records in her *Testament*, "that we should persevere always in holy poverty."

The nuns support the friars' active apostolate with contemplative prayer. The brethren in turn beg alms for the Poor Ladies. When at one point a pope forbids visitation by friars assigned as chaplains unless given permission for the particular occasion, Clare decrees that neither will the men who regularly beg for them be allowed in the cloister to deliver the daily bread and other contributions. She argues that the spiritual food provided by chaplains is just as necessary to the women as the material kind. The order is quickly rescinded.

Though prayer serves as the focus of the nuns' vocation, Clare believes in manual work too. The women do household chores, cultivate a small vegetable garden, spin cloth to make altar linens and nurse the sick brought to them, including any lepers Francis might send to have their sores bathed and bandaged.

Clare's charitable impulses developed early. As a child she found ways to give her own meals to the poor on many occasions. And when converted by Francis, she resourcefully managed to distribute her entire inheritance to the needy. (She may have had an ally in her devout mother, Ortolano. Sometime after the death of Favarone, she, too, joined the Poor Ladies. So did Clare's youngest sister, Beatrice.)

When the order is formalized in 1215, a reluctant Clare, for she is scarcely twenty-one, accedes to Francis' naming her abbess. (She calls herself "the little plant of the most blessed Father Francis."[2]) Unlike the traditional religious superior of the time, Clare sees her role of abbess as one of servant to her sisters. Among the ways she does this is by washing the feet of the lay sisters, those nuns who are permitted outside the cloister to attend to convent errands. No ritual foot washing this is, for the sisters come back from walking barefoot along muddy country lanes and garbage-strewn city streets. One of Francis' first friars, Thomas of Celano, in his biography of Clare reports, "She never shrank from any menial task, so that at the table she usually poured water on the hands of the Sisters, assisted those who were sitting, and served those who were eating. She herself washed and cleansed the commodes of the sick Sisters, making nothing of it, minding not the filth or the odor."[3]

Where the welfare of her Poor Ladies is concerned, Clare shows maternal solicitude: going through the dormitory at night to pull blankets over sleeping sisters, allowing feather pillows for the ailing and ordering woolen stockings for those especially sensitive to the cold. In the early years Clare herself practices austerities she warns the others against: rigorous fasting (three days a week she eats nothing), wearing a hair shirt (a practice dating to her pre-convent days), sleeping on vine twigs with a stone for a pillow.

When worried nuns tell Francis what she's been doing, he insists that she moderate her ways, making sure first of all that she has a mattress and pillow stuffed with straw. Clare's mortifications can only be understood in terms of her ardent love for God and the matching desire to express it in heroic fashion. Both Clare and Francis will realize too late, when their health begins to fail, that they have overdone a good thing.

Clare's love takes in all of God's creation, including her pet cat. She has a hole cut in the refectory door of the convent so that the cat can come in for meals. (The animal's special entrance is still pointed out to visitors at San Damiano.)

In 1219 the two persons dearest to Clare's heart each take leave of Assisi. Her sister Agnes is sent to a religious community near Florence to instill the spirit of the Poor Ladies. This is the first of more than a hundred similar monasteries to be established during Clare's lifetime. The two sisters will not see each other again until the abbess is on her deathbed years later.

Francis departs, too, on an impetuous journey to the Holy Land in hopes of converting the Saracens to Christianity. He leaves other friars in charge at home. The brotherhood has now grown to five thousand members, many of whom feel that Francis' ideal is simply no longer practical. While he is away, they set about "regularizing" the friars into a more traditional structure, acquiring property and eliminating absolute poverty. They attempt to do the same with the Poor Ladies, but Clare will have none of it.

When Francis returns from an unsuccessful mission, with his health already deteriorating, and discovers that a new rule for Franciscans is about to be approved, he in effect withdraws from administration of the order. In 1225 he retires for nearly two months to San Damiano, where Clare has a hut built in the garden for the ailing Francis. Amid her favorite flowers—lilies, roses and violets—he composes "The Canticle of the Creatures" and also a hymn in praise of the Poor Ladies. After this peaceful interlude, he receives the stigmata, and Clare makes him a special pair of slippers to relieve the pain of the wounds.

Before his death in 1226 he asks that she remain faithful to the poverty they both believe in. She will keep the promise despite the best attempts of several powerful popes who, though they admire the abbess tremendously, wish her to modify the Rule at least a little. After all, the friars have done so.

Two years after Francis' death Pope Gregory IX, who had been a friend in his cardinal days, insists on endowing the Second Order with land and a building. In a celebrated interview he suggests releasing her from the "absolute" part of her vow of poverty to ease her conscience about accepting property. Clare refuses to accept anything and tells the pope: "Holy Father, never do I wish to be released in any way from the following of Christ,"[4] Gregory finds himself yielding, and in a subsequent letter to her (September 17, 1228) makes it official: "We confirm your resolution to live in the utmost poverty, and by the authority of this present letter we confirm to you the privilege that no one can coerce you to receive possessions."[5]

Yet the struggle is not over, for Gregory and his successor will persist in attempts to make Clare compromise, to amend the Poor

Ladies' gospel form of life, giving them rules less demanding. It is no easy task to oppose a pope, no matter how well-meaning he is. (A few years before her death Clare begins to put into writing a Rule based on what she and Francis had agreed to long ago.)

Even without the beloved Francis as ally, life must go on. Clare continues as abbess notwithstanding her growing infirmities. On occasion the nuns have to lift her up so that she can spin wool and linen. During several harrowing incidents, however, it is Clare who gives her sisters support—of a moral kind.

The first occasion is when Assisi gets caught in the crossfire between the Papal States of central Italy and Frederick II of Germany. In the political maze of the times, the emperor also has dominion over Sicily, where his subjects include Saracens (as Arab Muslims were called then), who had once controlled that island. Frederick recruits them into his army. While on mission for him in the Umbrian hills, they go on a pillaging raid. As they scale the outer walls of San Damiano late at night, their blood-curdling cries terrify the sisters, who rush to Clare's sickbed. Helped up, she prays, then turns to the women and says, "My sisters and daughters, do not fear because God will be with us and the enemies will not be able to harm us.... I will be your hostage so that no hurt shall touch you. Should the enemies come so far put me in front of them."[6] Ready to die for them, she takes the silver box containing the Blessed Sacrament to an open window. By now the Saracens have placed a ladder against the building itself but, at sight of the majestic Clare, they suddenly, miraculously, take flight.

The following year imperial soldiers are again in the area, planning to plunder Assisi. As the citizens organize to defend themselves, Clare and her nuns pray for deliverance of the city. These soldiers also unaccountably flee in disorder. The people of Assisi are forever grateful to the Poor Ladies for the strength of their prayers.

A feeling for the kind of prayer life that went on at San Damiano can be gained from Thomas of Celano's contemporary description of the abbess who led them: "When [Clare] returned with joy from holy prayer, she brought with her burning words from the fire of the altar of the Lord, which enkindled the hearts of the sisters." They marveled indeed that such "sweetness came from her lips while her face shone more radiantly than usual."[7]

Clare's years of praying that the Franciscan ideal may be preserved by her Second Order find fulfillment two days before her death, when the Rule she has written to confirm absolute poverty receives official papal approval. When the document is delivered to her, eyewitnesses say that she "takes it in her hands and places it on her mouth and kisses it." An anonymous note written on the back of the parchment says, "The blessed Clare touched and kissed this Bull [Papal Letter] out of great devotion many, many times."[8]

The original written text of Clare's Rule, lost for centuries, was rediscovered in 1893 by the abbess at the monastery. She found the precious parchment wrapped in one of Clare's habits and hidden in a reliquary box. It is more than a footnote in history, for the document signifies one of Clare's greatest achievements: She was the first woman in the history of the church to write her own Rule for religious life—and have it officially approved.

ᴀғᴛᴇʀᴡᴀʀᴅ

For more than forty years, until her death in 1253, Clare was shut away from the world. She was cloistered but not sheltered, for popes came to visit her at San Damiano and queens wrote to her for advice. Agnes of Bohemia was the first member of royalty to enter a Poor Ladies community after turning down offers of marriage from such suitors as Frederick II. Some of Clare's letters to Agnes on the spiritual life reveal in her own words how love permeated her prayer. (These letters are regarded as gems of spiritual literature.) Physically enclosed, Clare's spirit soared.

The process for her canonization began two months after her death. Two years later, in declaring Clare a saint, Pope Alexander IV describes her thus: "She was kept inside, and remained outside. Clare was hidden, yet her way of life was open. Clare kept silent, but her fame cried out. She was concealed in a cell, but she was taught in the cities. It is no wonder that so bright and gleaming a light could not be hidden, but must shine forth and give clear light in the Lord's house."[9]

Together with Francis, Clare refreshed the entire church, and the effects are still being felt. The achievements of one can never be mentioned without the other. Theirs is one of the outstanding examples in Christianity of a pure and perfect friendship. One suspects that Clare was most in Francis' mind when he once told some friars his feelings toward the Poor Ladies: "Do not believe, dearest brothers, that I do not love them perfectly."[10]

The Franciscan ideal—preserving the heart of the gospel through loving service—was Clare's gift to Francis and the church. She never failed her cherished friend. The Friars Minor and Poor Clares (as her order came to be called) gave rise to a Third Order: people of their day who wanted to live in the Franciscan way even though circumstances prohibited their entering a religious community. First called Brothers and Sisters of Penance, these groups of lay men and women spread rapidly across Europe. (Queen Elizabeth of Hungary was among the first members.) The importance of this to the spiritual life of the laity in the Middle Ages was immense.

Blessed Lord,

Through her form of life,
Clare held firm to her dream
Of following the gospel way,
Her absolutely poverty
Made her spiritually rich.

I begin to write
My own form of life;
And ponder long
On how to fulfill my dream.
Amen.

13 : Clare of Assisi

THE FOURTEENTH CENTURY

Catherine of Siena

Background

The fourteenth century began on a note of celebration when Pope Boniface VIII declared the year 1300 a "Jubilee Year" for Rome. (The nightmare of the Black Death still lay ahead; it first appeared in 1347.) Pilgrims from around Christendom were invited to visit the Roman shrines and churches dedicated to Saints Peter and Paul—and leave their offerings. For Boniface saw the occasion as a great way to raise funds. Failing to reckon with rising nationalistic feelings in Europe, he also envisioned putting papal power on display.

In his dealings with secular rulers Boniface knew how to antagonize—especially Philip IV, king of France. That was a mistake, for in a contest of power, Philip would come out ahead of the sixty-eight-year-old Boniface.

Soon after Boniface's death, Philip managed to get a French pope elected—one who preferred living closer to home. The papal court was therefore removed to Avignon which, though not then officially part of France but situated just across its border, fell under the domination of the king. Thus began what history terms the "Babylonian Captivity," during which the papacy lost not only its international standing in temporal affairs but its moral authority, too. (Babylon referred to the worldliness of Avignon. Some Franciscans coined the term.) Transferring the court moreover proved an expensive proposition. It required building anew a city worthy of the court, adding taxes on religious orders as well as the laity. This did nothing to increase a pope's popularity.

Great spiritual lights such as Dante Alighieri (who was also deeply involved in the politics of Florence) and Birgitta of Sweden tried to persuade the papacy to return to Rome, but met with only short lived success. For a brief moment in time, it seemed that their prayers were answered. In 1367 one pope did return. Urban V had hoped that with apostolic Rome as his base, he could legitimately negotiate to heal the split with the Eastern church. When that failed, and civil disorder persisted in Italy, with Rome itself as unstable as ever, Urban went back to Avignon after an absence of three years. He died a few months later.

While in the long run neither Dante nor Birgitta managed to achieve their goal, but they proved something valuable: that at a very low point for the institutional church Christianity could yet soar in spirituality. In one of those marvelous paradoxes of church history, the fourteenth century witnessed an unparalleled flowering of the mystic life among individual Christians.

Avignon, June 18, 1376

Preceded by her reputation, the young woman and her party from Siena go ashore. A small boat has taken them up the Rhone River on the last stage of their journey from Italy. Standing on the quay, they can see the towers and spires of the palace and the other magnificent buildings belonging to the papal court, which has been in residence here ever since 1309—much too long, in Catherine's opinion. (Clement V had remained in France after his election in 1305, subsequently moving to Avignon.)

When received by the pope two days later, she gives no sign of being overawed by her surroundings or by the man she faces. Catherine has written Gregory XI often enough in the past, addressing him at times as *"dolce babbo"* ("sweetest father"), imploring him always to move back to Italy, to the Papal States, where the head of the church belongs. Meeting her now in person, Gregory waits to hear what this frail, impassioned woman has to say.

Catherine comes directly to the point: "To the glory of Almighty God I am bound to say that I smelt the stink of the sins which flourish in the papal court while I was still at home in my own town more sharply than those who have practised them, and do practise them, every day here."[1] (She has had several days to observe.)

Her spiritual adviser serves as interpreter, since the pope is French and Catherine speaks only her native Tuscan. Lack of formal education and lack of an aristocratic background (Catherine's father was a cloth-dyer) are not enough to hold her back, however.

Gregory recognizes the truth of her words as well as the obvious holiness that animates her. Despite her urgent call to action, he vacillates. For pious though the pope may be, courage characteristically fails him. There are just too many pressures coming from the powerful French king, the luxury-loving French cardinals and the vast number of hangers-on who have no desire to leave the opulence of Avignon for the ruins called Rome. Undeterred by such formidable forces, Catherine continues to argue the issue. Her beloved church is in peril and she feels called by God to do what she can to save it.

In the nearly seventy years since a French king managed to shift the papal court to Avignon, the papacy has been reduced to a political tool. In a century marked by the Hundred Years' War between England and France, recurrent epidemics of the Black Death throughout Europe and interminable feuding among Italy's various city-states, Christian society needs spiritual guidance more than ever. Yet even the monasteries, Catherine tells Gregory, are "stables of swine." The only way the pope can purify the church is by leaving the corrupting influence of Avignon and thus escape domination by kings. Back in his own Papal States, Gregory will be free to act independently and achieve reform.

He must think about it.

Meanwhile, when Catherine is not engaged in efforts to persuade, she prays. And when her devotions are public—as at Mass—she attracts the considerable curiosity of the women at court, who include both relatives of the prelates and their mistresses. Some take Catherine seriously; others seem afraid of this reformer and still others make fun of her.

Revered as a mystic by the band of disciples who have accompanied her to Avignon, she is gifted with visions and subject to trances. Seeing her in the chapel one day, prostrate on the floor after falling into a trance, one young woman who is married to the pope's nephew sticks a large needle into Catherine's foot to determine whether it is really true that the mystic feels nothing while divinely transported. After regaining consciousness, Catherine begins to experience so much pain that she is unable to stand on the wounded foot for several days.

At the end of three months Gregory succumbs to her logic, and starts the journey to Rome. At the port of Marseilles, Catherine makes sure he boards the ship for Genoa. She and her companions apparently take the overland route. At Genoa he arranges to meet her again secretly for added encouragement to go on. At long last she is free to return to Siena, where she regularly nurses the sick, assists the poor and visits those in prison. This Catherine does in spite of persistent ill health—always doing what she believes necessary, a trait that has marked her since childhood.

Twenty-fourth of the twenty-five children born to Jacopo and Monna Lapa Benincasa, Catherine made a vow of virginity at the age of seven. Even then, the happy-natured little girl showed evidence of a strong spiritual bent. Her parents allowed her to fast and do penances as she chose, for they were devout themselves. But when she reached the marriageable age of thirteen, the heretofore obedient Catherine absolutely refused to marry the young man Jacopo had in mind for her. In hopes of bringing about a change, he and Monna Lapa began imposing menial household chores on their adored daughter, leaving her little time for prayer. The single-minded girl found she could retreat into her interior "cell" as she worked. And rather than hold a grudge against the family (for brothers and sisters took to taunting her), she waited on them as though they were the Holy Family. Seeing the very best in everyone was to become a lifelong habit for her.

Finally the parents relented and, at sixteen, Catherine was accepted as a member of the local Dominican Third Order, even though its membership was then ordinarily restricted to widows. These tertiaries took no monastic vows but lived in their own homes, dedicating themselves to charitable works. As their badge of identification, the women wore a coarse white robe similar to that of the Dominicans' black mantle. For this reason, they were sometimes referred to as the *Mantellate*.

With the approval of her spiritual director, Catherine spent the next three years in the solitude of her little room: praying and fasting, doing sacred reading, sleeping on a bare board and going out only to attend Mass. (During that time she learned to read.) Never one to neglect friends, though, she wove wreaths of flowers that she sent them as greetings.

Hearing a call from God to begin her apostolic labors, Catherine reentered the world. Her kind of holiness, her joy in serving others, soon attracted a following. Two of her original disciples were sister members of the Third Order, educated women who wrote Catherine's letters for her in the early years since Catherine did not yet know how to write; but male disciples from all ranks of life joined her band too. Jacopo Benincasa granted use of the family home as the base of operations.

The neighbors talked, of course, when they saw numbers of men going in and out of the Benincasa house at all hours of the day and night, and young Catherine freely going about the town with them. She had no time to worry about talk (which did eventually subside); she was too busy not only with missions of charity but also meeting a growing demand for her services as a peacemaker, healing rifts within families and between feuding families, a particular problem of the time.

Shortly after her father's death, a revolution broke out in the region. It lasted just long enough to affect the family fortunes as well as the local economy. Catherine's brothers had to look elsewhere for work and somehow, out of all that large family, she was the one to assume responsibility for the care of their mother. Thereafter, when Catherine traveled on peacemaking errands, Monna Lapa was found among the company of disciples.

There was little time for travel in 1374, though, for the Black Death—bubonic plague—made its second appearance in Siena. During an earlier epidemic, soon after Catherine's birth, Siena had lost one-third of its population. The disease continued to ravage Europe in waves, decimating the ranks of clergymen (which accounts for some of the church's problems). The lower clergy willingly worked among the afflicted despite the danger. When Catherine joined in the effort, she met a priest, Raymond of Capua, who became her spiritual director and cherished friend for the rest of her short life. As the plague intensified, death carts made the rounds of the city each day to pick up the latest victims. Among them were two brothers and a sister of Catherine, and eight of the eleven grandchildren her mother had been raising.

When the epidemic ended, Catherine resumed her role of diplomat, answering first a call from the citizens of Pisa. Having shown an ability to reconcile feuding parties, she now got requests for help in settling differences between the various city-states of the Italian peninsula. Vying with each other for economic and political power, these independent republics—and the papacy too—hired mercenary soldiers to wage their wars. Prelates and others in authority found it almost impossible to believe that a young woman could be capable of conducting negotiations—until they met Catherine. While in Pisa, she heard that some of the cities were forming a league. To her sorrow, this newfound unity came about in order to fight the Holy See.

At the heart of the trouble was the city of Florence, at odds with the pope, who angrily placed Florence under interdict, ordering that its trade be cut off—the lifeblood of Florentine wealth. And here Catherine got involved. In 1376 the Florentines ask her to intercede for them, and she heads for Avignon—bringing us back to the start of our story.

While the officials of Florence mean only to use her as a pawn in a political game and, in effect, to leave her in the lurch when their own aims are met, an undismayed Catherine takes advantage of the circumstances to achieve her own long-held dream of getting the pope back to Rome.

But once there, the thoroughly French Pope Gregory discovers Rome is not to his liking and, as a consequence, develops a certain coolness toward Catherine. While working among the needy again in Siena—and in her spare time, founding a monastery for women—she gets a call from the pope asking her to go to Florence once more. Scarcely has she arrived there in early March, 1378, when news comes of Gregory's death. But a new pope, Urban VI, an Italian, is named within ten days, and he wants her to carry on.

With pro-papal and anti-papal factions doing violence to each other in Florence, Catherine gets blamed for the excesses of those who champion the pope. She and some friends are confronted in a garden one day by a mob demanding with drawn swords "that cursed Catherine." She steps forward and tells them to do what they wish to her, but asks that they not harm her friends. The leader of the group then advises her to flee. She adamantly refuses, adding that she is ready to die if it will promote peace. The mob instead retreats. Catherine remains in the vicinity of Florence until an acceptable peace settlement has been concluded.

Catherine returns to Siena with her faithful disciples, who call her "Mamma" regardless of their age. Some of her male disciples have by now been serving in a secretarial role to handle the voluminous correspondence (almost four hundred letters still exist) addressed to popes and princes and many others.

In October, 1377, Catherine begins a year's work, composing what would become her masterpiece, *The Dialogue*, recording her conversation with God. It consists of ten sections in which she presents four petitions to which God responds, followed by her thanksgiving. (Catherine places great value on the power of intercessory prayer.) So fast does her mind work that she keeps three secretaries busy taking dictation. (*The Dialogue* has been

WOMEN IN CHURCH HISTORY

described as "the love song of the soul and God, of Catherine and her Beloved."[2])

While working on the book, she learns that the French have elected a rival pope. Pope Urban, though morally above reproach, has been proving utterly tactless in his dealings with people. Catherine writes him: "For the love of Christ crucified... restrain a little those hasty movements of your nature."[3]

Urban summons Catherine to Rome to help rally support in his favor. Spending the last months of her life in Rome, she sends letter after letter to European rulers and prelates of the opposition party. Trying to save the papacy from disaster, she also addresses the Sacred College of Cardinals, urging them to have faith. When she concludes, Urban says to them: "See, brothers, how guilty we must appear to God because we are without courage. This little woman puts us to shame. And when I call her a little woman, I do not do so out of scorn, but because her sex is by nature fearful; but see how we tremble while she is strong and calm, and see how she consoles us with her words."[4]

Catherine foresees schism facing the church. Her always fragile health fails rapidly. She suffers two strokes and—some say—a broken heart. Raymond of Capua says of her: "Catherine carried the whole church in her heart."[5] Near the end, she tells her disciples: "Love one another, my children, love one another! for by this shall you show that you have had me and own me for mother."[6]

Afterward

When Catherine died at thirty-three, she genuinely believed herself a failure. Yet she had single-handedly changed the course of history by ending the Babylonian Captivity. Had this great peacemaker lived, perhaps the Great Schism that rent the church might have been headed off. Instead, it would eventually produce three popes, each one asking for obedience as well as contributions.

Only a general council called at Constance finally ended the long schism in 1417.

In her brief day Catherine was the most powerful woman in Europe. Like Hildegard of Bingen before her, she served as conscience of the church when it was in dire need of one. The people of Siena realized her worth, venerating Monna Lapa (who lived to the age of ninety) as the mother of a saint. Two of her male disciples went on to become heads of their orders: Dominican Raymond of Capua and Carthusian Stefano Maconi.

Institutional problems of the church aside, the fourteenth century of Christianity was distinguished for its surge of mystical development, and Catherine was one of the most outstanding in a line of outstanding mystics. The theology presented in her brilliant *Dialogue*, considered a jewel in Italian religious literature, eventually earned for this "unlettered" woman the title "Doctor of the Church"—a title given to only two other women in history. Catherine and Teresa of Avila received the honor in 1970. Thérèse of Lisieux was named in 1997. Above all, Catherine showed what heights could be attained by one individual grounded in prayer and motivated by love of God and humanity.

LORD OF ALL,

THOUGH SHE SOARED TO MYSTICAL HEIGHTS,
CATHERINE NEVER FORGOT
GOD IS THERE TO LISTEN
TO OUR PRAYERS OF PETITION,
AS HER DIALOGUE SO CLEARLY SHOWS.

WHILE PRAYERS OF INTERCESSION
TAKE US TO OUR KNEES, NOT HEIGHTS,

In a very mystical way
They bind us to God and each other.
Amen.

THE FIFTEENTH CENTURY

CATHERINE OF GENOA

BACKGROUND

Through both trade and the Crusades, Europeans had made close contact with the Islamic civilization of the East, one far advanced in science and the arts. Moreover, Muslim scholars had been busy rediscovering and preserving the classics of Greek and Roman antiquity. New ideas (regular bathing was one) as well as ancient learning found their way back to Europe, triggering the Renaissance.

It started in Florence, the city-state emerging as the hub of international banking. While other parts of Europe were developing into nations, Italian cities remained independent republics. The wealthiest families in each city-state assumed control, often passing down power to succeeding generations.

Prosperous Florentine bankers were among the first to invest in the arts. Such was the spirit of the times in Florence that the most talked-about event there in 1401 was a design competition for a set of sculptured doors for the town baptistery.

In the preoccupation with creating art and making money, scarcely a European brow was lifted when Constantinople appealed to the West for help as the Ottoman Turks besieged the city. The last official Crusade to defeat the infidels was long past, and so was interest in mounting another one, even though Pope Pius II offered to lead it himself. He tried in vain to rally Western rulers to the cause. Virtually the only response came from the merchants of Genoa, anxious that something be done lest they lose their trading rights in Constantinople in a Turkish takeover. Clearly that was not response enough. Constantinople, the last bastion of Eastern Christendom, fell in 1453.

REPUBLIC OF GENOA, JANUARY 13, 1463

With "the utmost repugnance" Catherine Fiesca signs the marriage contract. From all appearances, the groom, Giuliano Adorno, shares her sentiments. Not made in heaven, this marriage is rather arranged by Catherine's older brother, head of the family since their father's death a few years earlier. The wedding ceremony itself will be celebrated at a later date in the Cathedral of San Lorenzo, across the way from the Fieschi Palazzo, where the couple will reside for the first two years.

What the marriage actually celebrates is a binding-up of political wounds. The two families that Catherine and Giuliano represent have long been on opposite, warring sides, and the resultant civil disturbances threatened to undermine Genoese prosperity if the situation is not resolved.

No matter how sixteen-year-old Catherine looks upon the arrangement, tradition dictates that her brother's authority may not be questioned. So little heed is paid to her feelings, in fact, that no one bothers to tell her until the date and place of the ceremony have already been set.

She and young Giuliano come from similar backgrounds of wealth and social position, but they are otherwise totally unsuited. She, quiet and of a penitential nature, had attempted at thirteen to enter a convent but was refused because of her age. He, hot-tempered and self-indulgent, finds her tastes disagreeable, though for the most part he seems scarcely to give his wife a second thought. During the next ten years, he is often absent and unfaithful as well, as he later confesses.

Catherine's first reaction is to retire even more, redoubling her austerities. After a time she and Giuliano move from her mother's to take up residence at his palazzo. She spends lonely winters there and lonely summers at his country place on the Riviera, about six miles from Genoa. Neglected by her husband, Catherine also feels abandoned by God.

In the succeeding five years, yielding to pressure from family and friends, she resumes social activities in keeping with her position in one of the leading families of Genoa. But she finds this a meaningless kind of existence and sinks deeper into despondency.

In mounting distress Catherine goes one day in March, 1474, to a nearby convent where her older sister Limbania is a nun. Limbania persuades her to talk to the chaplain. But hardly has she set foot in the chapel than the priest is momentarily called away.

Years later she will confide to her closest friend what happens in the short interval alone. As her friend describes it:

> [H]er heart was pierced by so sudden and immense a love of God, accompanied by so penetrating a sight of her miseries and sins and of His goodness, that she was near falling to the ground. And in a transport of pure and all-purifying love, she was drawn away from the miseries of the world;

and as it were beside herself, kept crying out within herself: "No more world; no more sins." And at that moment she felt, that had she had in her possession a thousand worlds, she would have thrown them all away.[1]

When the chaplain returns, Catherine can only manage to excuse herself and postpone the confession to a later time.

Overcome by the love God has revealed, she shuts herself up in her room for several days, during which time she has a vision of Christ. Following that, Catherine gives away all her fashionable clothes, makes a general confession, becomes a daily communicant—an extraordinarily rare practice then—and embarks on a lengthy penitential period. Always trying to be inconspicuous, she will walk a mile out of town to receive the Eucharist so that friends will not see her and wonder. From this instantaneous, total conversion of heart, Catherine will never once waver.

In the autumn of that same year Giuliano experiences a revelation of his own: the high cost of a dissipated lifestyle. He sells the country place and leases out the palazzo in town. A now remorseful husband confesses the existence of his natural daughter, Thobia. Apparently already knowing about her, Catherine assures him of her forgiveness.

Despite financial losses, sufficient income remains in order to live quite comfortably. Yet the two, at last in accord, decide instead to move into a little house in a neighborhood of working-class poor near the Hospital of the Pammatone. Both agree also to a life of chastity from then on. Giuliano joins the Third Order of Saint Francis. Though Catherine feels strongly influenced by Franciscan teaching—particularly as expressed in the writings of mystic and poet Jacopone da Todi—she never shows an inclination to become a tertiary herself.

One day a friar tells her that he, as a religious, can love God better, chiding her for having "married the world." Catherine gets so wrought up over his remarks, her hair comes undone and falls about her shoulders as, face aflame, she exclaims that if his habit would help her to love God better she would tear it from his back.

She has far from married the world. During the four years immediately following her conversion, she has spent six hours a day in prayer, coming from prayer "joyous and rosy-faced." As part of the fasting regime she continues for many years, she abstains from any solid food every Lent and Advent. Her friends marvel that during these fasting periods, Catherine is more active in pursuing good works, stronger and even more radiant than usual. It can only be explained as a special grace from God.

No longer does Catherine doubt the meaning of existence. She and Giuliano together attend to the needs of the sick and poor in their neighborhood in addition to caring for patients in the hospital. Giuliano has never before worked at an occupation. The fastidious Catherine must overcome feelings of squeamishness when she cleans filth-ridden houses in the slum area and takes dirty, vermin-covered clothing home for washing.

In 1479 they move again, this time into two small rooms at the hospital, where both continue to perform even the most menial nursing chores, still at no pay. Catherine takes delight in singing lighthearted verses of her own composition in which she speaks to the Lord of love. Though she is a woman of powerful intellect and is generally viewed as rather sober-minded, the little rhymes reveal another facet of her nature:

> Dost thou wish that I should show
> All God's Being thou mayst know?
> Peace is not found of those who do not with Him go.[2]

In the original Italian, the sound is melodious.

After eleven years of service, Catherine is appointed hospital matron, that is, director of the institution. When an epidemic of deadly fever strikes in the early spring of 1493 and lasts until the end of the summer, 80 percent of Genoa's citizens die. As matron, Catherine organizes medical staffing, supplemented by volunteer priests and tertiaries. To handle the overflow of patients, she has rows of sailcloth tents set up on the hospital's grounds. To her falls the task of bringing order out of a chaotic situation and easing the fears of panic-stricken victims. She is unsparing in her care for the sick.

Most who can afford to—that is, the wealthy class—flee the city while the epidemic rages. One who stays behind, Ettore Vernazza, a twenty-three-year-old lawyer, enlists as an aide. When he and Catherine meet, it marks the start of a close, enduring friendship—though it very nearly misses being a long one. For in a compassionate gesture, she kisses a dying patient, contracts the disease and almost dies from the fever herself.

In 1496 Catherine's health begins to fail, marked primarily by great weakness of body. She therefore resigns her post as matron, although she still lives at the hospital and works when possible. A year later after a long illness Giuliano dies. In his will he asks that Catherine see to the continued support of his daughter Thobia and the child's mother as in the past. This Catherine takes care of with a characteristically generous spirit.

At this point her life takes a new turn. She suffers from an illness doctors can neither explain nor find treatment for (she speaks of "great burnings" on occasion). But Catherine recognizes it as nervous in origin. As the illness progresses and makes it impossible to work, she is free to spend much time with the circle of disciples who have been drawn to her and regard her as their spiritual mother.

Prominent among the men are Ettore Vernazza, along with Dom Cattaneo Marabotto, a priest appointed rector at the hospital around 1499. The latter becomes Catherine's spiritual director during these last years (until now, she has made her mystical pilgrimage on her own). His direction consists essentially in giving back to her, when asked, the words of counsel she gave him on some previous occasion.

Among her female disciples, a favorite is her cousin Tommasina. The two are the same age and share religious interests as well as intellectual pursuits. (The widowed Tommasina becomes first a Dominican tertiary, then a nun.) But they differ in personality. Tommasina likes to tease her more intensely tuned cousin, saying one day with a twinkle in her eyes, that after all the mortifications, what if Catherine had a change of heart? Catherine's passionate response is swift: "If I were to turn back, I would wish that my eyes might be put out!"[3]

Tommasina, a gifted artist, is believed by some to have painted the portrait of Catherine that hangs in the Municipal Hospital of Genoa. The painting depicts its subject with a sensitive mouth but strong chin, oval face of delicate complexion, gray-blue eyes and thick dark hair.

Catherine has always been passionate about everything. In the final years the love that permeates Catherine's life encompasses God's other creations as well as humanity. Friends say that "if an animal were killed or a tree cut down, she could hardly bear to see them lose that being which God had given them."[4]

She has the envied capacity to appreciate the sacrament of the moment: finding God in the present, plumbing the depths of experience whether that be suffering, the commonplace or the sweetest peace. God, for Catherine—from moment of conversion to moment of death—is "Boundless Love."

Dom Marabotto and Ettore Vernazza team up to collect their spiritual mother's profound sayings and to record her life. Among her teachings, the treatise on purgatory presents one of the church's most illuminating views on the subject—a classic in

Catholic theology. Drawing from her own experience, Catherine interprets the way of purgation for the soul in this life or after death. In uplifting words Catherine declares:

> There is no joy save that in paradise to be compared to the joy of the souls in purgatory. This joy increases day by day because of the way in which the love of God corresponds to that of the soul, since the impediment to that love is worn away daily. This impediment is the rust of sin. As it is consumed, the soul is more and more open to God's love.... The more rust of sin is consumed by fire, the more the soul responds to that love, and its joy increases.[5]

This treatise is only part of Catherine's larger doctrine on the all-embracing goodness of God, but it is due to receive greater emphasis because of a controversy involving Martin Luther that happens shortly after her death in 1510. The following chapter explains the reason why.

In her last days Catherine tries to describe to her disciples exactly what mystical joy means. "Oh, would that I could tell you what my heart feels!... I cannot find words appropriate to so great a love. But this I can say with truth, that if of what my heart feels one drop were to fall into hell, hell itself would turn into eternal life!"[6]

AFTERWARD

Evelyn Underhill, a classic authority and writer on mysticism, described Catherine of Genoa as "one of the deepest gazers into the secrets of Eternal Love that the history of Christian mysticism contains."[7]

This magnificent soul attained the summit of spirituality in her own unique way—as a layperson independent of any affiliation—and even went without a spiritual director until the last years of her life. Like many other mystics, Catherine combined her full prayer life with one of active Christian charity.

Though her family tree included two popes (Innocent IV and Hadrian V) and one of her cousins was a prominent cardinal, she never showed a hint of interest in ecclesiastical affairs. Contrast the works of Genoa and the works of Rome: While Catherine was nursing plague victims and cleaning house for the sick and poor of her city, popes of that era concentrated on the business of the Italian Renaissance, promoting the splendors of art and architecture. This occupied their energies to the extent that the murmurings of discontent across Christendom were either ignored or dismissed as being of no consequence.

In the quest for beauty one pope's papal crown cost two million francs. Another, Alexander VI (one of the notorious Borgias), added not only to the glory of Rome but to the bank accounts of his children and grandchildren as he distributed church wealth among them. To pay for all the luxuries, indulgences as well as ecclesiastical offices were sold, and the murmurings grew to rumblings.

Still, the papacy neglected—indeed, aggravated—the conditions that would lead to the Protestant Revolt soon after Catherine's death.

In her quiet way Catherine provided a needed spirituality for her time and, in her gospel kind of humanitarianism, she did "something beautiful for God."

BOUNDLESS LOVE,

VULNERABLE AS ANYONE MIGHT BE
TO THE WOUNDS OF INSENSITIVITY,
EVEN OF MISDEEDS,
YET CATHERINE'S GENEROUS HEART
ERASED IT ALL.

MERCIFUL LORD, HELP ME
TO FORGET AS WELL AS FORGIVE;
NO HALFWAY MEASURES
WILL DO.
AMEN.

THE SIXTEENTH CENTURY

TERESA OF AVILA

BACKGROUND

When Martin Luther posted his ninety-five theses on the church door in Wittenberg, it was not his intention to challenge the structure of the entire Catholic church. Rather, he was just following normal procedure among intellectuals wishing to debate an issue. Others had been campaigning for reform before this Augustinian monk, but circumstances made him the catalyst of the explosion of unhappiness over the abuses and corruption in the church.

It happened that Rome needed money again, this time to help pay for the rebuilding of St. Peter's. Selling indulgences promising a remission of punishment for sins to the faithful of Europe offered a practical solution. (According to church teachings, indulgences could lessen a soul's time spent in purgatory.)

Unfortunately for Rome, nationalistic feelings were by now particularly strong in Germany. Added to that, Germans had traditionally been opposed to seeing their money go off to Rome. When Luther made his protest against the sale of indulgences, a papal bull condemned his views and ordered him to appear for a hearing. He refused, perhaps afraid of being burned at the stake as a heretic. When Luther sought political support from German lords in the snowballing controversy, he got it. German rulers and the papacy were not new to confrontation. In 1521 Luther was excommunicated, even as his movement grew to include far more reform issues than the sale of indulgences.

In other countries, too, people were ready to revolt against papal authority. The English, for example, had long rebelled against Rome's interference in their internal politics. A dozen years after Luther's excommunication, Henry VIII became infatuated with a woman he thought capable of providing an heir to the throne; the papacy ruled against his remarriage and England set up its own church, free to make its own rules.

Spain, however, was in a different mood. With the conquest of Granada by Catholic forces in 1492, the whole of Spain returned to Christian rule, under King Ferdinand and Queen Isabella. That same year all Jews who refused to convert to Christianity were forcibly expelled. The Moors (Muslims from North Africa of Berber-Arab stock), who had occupied the Iberian Peninsula since the eighth century, were allowed to remain for a time, though always under suspicion and pressure to convert. They were finally expelled in the early 1600s. For the Spanish there was no question that the Catholic church was the sole answer to faith. The only question was: How exactly should that faith be lived?

AVILA, SPAIN, ALL SOULS' DAY, 1536

In the chill November dawn Teresa de Ahumada steals away from the family home, a younger brother accompanying her as far as the gate of the Carmelite Convent of the Incarnation beyond the city walls. After five years of indecision, the young woman has settled on becoming a nun. She is making the move without her father's consent, though, and that causes her great distress.

It is not as if religious dedication were the motivating factor behind her choice. Rather, an illness brought Teresa to the realization that life could be cut short; because of her frivolous ways, hell might be her fate. In her autobiography she later admits to being "afraid of marriage" (perhaps the result of observing her mother's steady decline in health after a number of pregnancies). But fun-loving Teresa also views the cloister as a kind of purgatory, though she concludes that purgatory is preferable to hell. As she says, "I saw that this was the best and safest state, and so, little by little, I determined to force myself to embrace it."[1]

The convent accepts twenty-one-year-old Teresa, and the following year she professes vows. Life at Incarnation is not without its compensations. Typical of religious communities then, visitors to the parlor, even gentlemen callers, are frequent—almost interminable, Teresa will eventually say—for the convent houses at least 130 nuns. Though some sleep in the dormitory, those who are well provided for by their families in terms of dowry enjoy private rooms. Because Teresa's father shortly comes around to her choice of vocation, she falls into the latter category. Those who can afford them feast on delicacies sent in, wear jewelry and make extended outside visits to family or friends.

A year after her profession, Teresa goes through a long period of illness marked by fainting fits and heart problems. When none of the doctors' ministrations help, she is sent for treatment to a *curandera*, or female healer, about forty miles from Avila. Her condition worsens and, after a severe cataleptic fit that leaves her unconscious and unmoving for four days, a grave is even dug for her. (Catalepsy may be either neurological or psychological in origin. If the latter, the consequent paralysis is sometimes attributed to hysteria. Some scholars speculate that Teresa's illness was psychological in nature, prompted by interior struggles over her spiritual life.) Through the intercession of Saint Joseph, as she believes, Teresa finally recovers sufficiently to return to the convent, though somewhat an invalid still. The effects of paralysis will stay with her for several years.

Beginning an attempt at serious prayer, she tries to find a confessor who will understand. Failing that, she turns for guidance to a book she read during the illness, Francisco de Osuna's *Third Spiritual Alphabet*. Osuna's words had made a strong impression upon her.

Although becoming increasingly aware of the shallowness of her interior life, Teresa remains torn between attempts at deeper prayer and the social distractions prevalent at the convent. She finds "neither any joy in God nor any pleasure in the world,"[2] she later reports. Her extroverted nature thrives on human company as well as its approval.

Her father's death in 1543 hits Teresa hard, for he was an important figure in her life, a source of both comfort and support. (Her mother had died when she was thirteen.)

For a dozen years after that, she continues on the "stormy sea," as she calls it. One day, chancing to look at a picture of the wounded Christ, Teresa is struck by the realization of all he had suffered and "how ill I had repaid him for those wounds that I felt as if my heart were breaking." In "floods of tears,"[3] she begs Christ for the strength to change.

As the forty-year-old nun ponders how best to serve God, to make amends, the answer seems clear: Follow the vocation given her as perfectly as possible. But to fulfill that vow required a spiritually oriented environment. Unfortunately, the Convent of the Incarnation—like so many others—had drifted far from the original contemplative ideal of the Carmelite Order.

Teresa's dream, which she and a few others discuss, revolves around the idea of a handful of nuns living apart, austerely, with strict enclosure, according to the order's Primitive Rule.

Still, the idea never gets beyond the talk stage until one day after Communion when Teresa relates, "the Lord gave me the most explicit commands to work for this aim," coupled with the promise that the convent she founds will "be a star giving out the most brilliant light."[4] (She has already begun to experience visions.)

When she broaches the subject with the local provincial of the order, he is in favor of the proposal at first. But once word of it leaks out, the fireworks start. With only a few exceptions, the sisters at Incarnation ridicule Teresa when they are not accusing her of insulting them by implying that their convent is not good enough. Some even suggest she be thrown into the convent prison cell. (Such cells were then a common way to deal with problem nuns in a religious community.) Teresa's friends fear far worse, for a rumor has begun circulating about the nun's having revelations. Should the dreaded Spanish Inquisition, always on the hunt for false mystics as well as for heretics, hear of this, it will likely investigate her. Punishment entails prison, torture and sometimes death. The Inquisition also seeks out *conversos*, Jews who ostensibly converted to Christianity but may continue in secret to practice their ancestral faith. Teresa's paternal grandfather had been a *converso*, and had moved his family (while Teresa's father was still a child) from Toledo to Avila to start a new life. Should this become known, Teresa would be receiving even more scrutiny.

The Carmelite nun's plan is denounced from the pulpits of Avila's churches. On one occasion, on an outing from the convent to visit her family, Teresa is in the congregation. Yet despite such opposition, Teresa doggedly goes ahead with negotiations to purchase a small house for the envisaged new convent. The day before signing of the deed, however, the provincial withdraws his permission. He simply cannot deal with all the commotion.

Throughout the struggle to establish a reform convent, Teresa does get ongoing support from Peter of Alcantara, a Franciscan working to instill in his own order more contemplative and penitential practices. The two had first met when she was looking for guidance in understanding the intellectual visions she was beginning to receive. (As Teresa would explain this type of vision in subsequent writings, the person does not see the Lord with the eyes but "is conscious that Jesus Christ stands by her side.... [T]his brings with it a special knowledge of God; a most tender love for Him results from being constantly in His company, while the desire of devoting one's whole being to His service is more fervent than any hitherto described."[5])

As troubles mount, Peter, having gone through it himself, tells her that opposition from good people is one of the worst trials in the world. And sure enough, she suffers the greatest pain when the confessor now assigned to her chastises her for causing scandal and orders no more talk or action regarding the project.

For the next five or six months, Teresa is in anguish—until an ecclesiastic new in authority proves to be on her side and directs the confessor to let the Spirit work through this crusading nun. To forestall the problems caused in the past by too much talk, it is agreed that henceforth the project must proceed in all secrecy.

Through her sister Juana arrangements are made to buy and furnish a house. Funds provided by several donors, including a well-to-do widow, are not quite sufficient to pay the workmen hired to make the modest house fit to live in. This time her brother Lorenzo comes to the rescue. (Throughout her life Teresa remains much involved in the welfare of her large family as they do with her undertakings.)

The biggest worry now is that her provincial—one of those kept in the dark—will discover what's going on and put a stop to it. On the advice of Peter of Alcantara and a few others, steps are taken by way of friends in high places in Rome to put the new convent directly under the protection of Avila's bishop, who is an unwavering supporter of reform. Approval from Rome arrives in July 1562. The following month a handful of nuns sharing Teresa's outlook move into St. Joseph's, as it is named, and within days the sisters at Incarnation, along with all of Avila, hear the news. The prioress at Incarnation immediately sends for Teresa.

"I went in the belief that I should at once be put in prison,"[6] she admits. The provincial makes an appearance at the interview too. After Teresa goes through a careful explanation of how she is only trying to strengthen the order, they begin to see things her way.

Next to be placated are city officials, for they feel Avila already has more than its share of poor religious houses dependent on local support. A report is forwarded to the Royal Council, and Teresa is forbidden to move to St. Joseph's until the matter is settled legally. She cannot understand the commotion brought on by the thought of twelve poor women plus a superior in one little house. The nuns already in residence begin their life of contemplative prayer regardless of the uproar. Teresa's choice of women, by the way, depends not at all on whether they have a dowry—one of the usual conditions for entry into religious life. It is their spirituality that counts.

In a complete turnaround, the people of Avila, seeing that the opposition has not been able to halt the convent's opening, conclude it must be the work of God. Legal proceedings are forthwith dropped, and a wave of public generosity provides alms even without any need for an appeal.

Teresa is now free to join her little community, which she likens to heaven. No class distinctions exist at St. Joseph's. All share in the chores—Teresa included, for she firmly believes in a rhythm of work and prayer. The nuns wear coarse brown habits and hempen sandals. (They are called Discalced—that is, "bare-footed"—Carmelites. Bare feet are a popular symbol of the day for the reform-minded, signifying poverty and simplicity.) But Teresa, who is always guided by good sense, makes sure her sisters have sandals.

Happier and healthier than ever before in the peacefulness of St. Joseph's, Teresa journeys to the heights of mystical prayer. Her superiors request that she write a spiritual autobiography, and after completing this, she begins work on an instructional book for prayer: *The Way of Perfection.*

In 1566 Teresa receives a promise from the Lord that soon she will "see great things." In April of the following year the prior-general of the Carmelite Order arrives on visitation from Rome. In answer to the Protestant Reformation, bishops of the church have come up with reforms of their own in a series of meetings (the Council of Trent, 1543–1563). The Carmelite head has come to Spain to make sure they are implemented. He likes what he sees at St. Joseph's and asks Teresa to do more of the same, giving her permission (although no money) to found not only more convents but also several reform houses for friars. She never worries about lack of funds but dives into the busiest period of her life.

While on a mission to Medina later that year Teresa becomes acquainted with a brilliant, highly educated Carmelite friar known to history as John of the Cross. Despite the difference in age (she is fifty-two and he, twenty-five), their rapport is immediate. She enlists John's help in working with men in the order.

Their names will be forever linked as a result of their joint accomplishments. During the years of working closely together the two obviously inspire each other, for each composes a masterpiece of literature: Teresa's *The Interior Castle* and John's *Spiritual Canticle*.

Their writing styles show the differences in their temperaments. She is witty and forceful; he is gentle and extremely sweet-natured. Her style is conversational, reflecting a natural exuberance, while his celebration of the love of God soars poetically.

When Teresa is recalled to Incarnation, John goes along as her confessor. This time, however, she will serve six years as prioress there to reform the convent—a prospect that upsets some nuns at first. Even while in charge of her old community, the energetic nun manages to go on founding additional convents. And the pattern of establishing St. Joseph's keeps repeating itself: first, opposition; then, aided by Teresa's persistence as well as charm, people coming around to accepting the inevitable.

To keep up with all that's happening, she conducts a voluminous correspondence. By the light of an oil lamp, Teresa writes her books as well as letters late at night, her only free time, her quill pen flying over the paper. Among her correspondents is Philip II, king of Spain, who likes her no-nonsense way. In this, Spain's "Golden Age," he is considered the most powerful man in Europe.

By 1577 the Carmelite reformer has become a national figure. The king's support for her is well-known—she needs it when opponents report some of her writings to the Spanish Inquisition. An appeal to the king gets her out of trouble. John of the Cross is not so lucky. Friars twice kidnap and imprison him in Toledo, where they regularly flog him, before he manages to escape. Clergy and religious who resist change can be brutal as well as intolerant.

Teresa somehow keeps her famous sense of humor despite

having her every move watched by persons who hope to catch her in a misstep. When one, for example, acts scandalized at seeing this nun of reforming zeal sit down to enjoy a meal of roast partridge prepared by the host, Teresa, never eccentric about religious practices, replies matter-of-factly, "There is a time for partridge and a time for penance."[7]

Her extensive journeys to found convents continue to the very end. Sometimes the great distances of Spain are traversed by mule, more often in a covered mule-cart made without springs but with heavy wooden wheels for the rough, at times impassable, roads. Whether in summer heat or the ice, snow and floods of winter, she travels not only with sisters as companions but also with an escort of laymen plus two or three of the clergy because of the danger of brigands. The inns are squalid and crowded with adventurers.

On what is to be her final trip, Teresa, now sixty-eight, becomes seriously ill at Alba de Tormes in the north-central part of the country. As death approaches, a priest asks if she would like her body returned to Avila for burial. "What?" she asks, still irrepressible. "Will they not give me a little earth here?"[8]

AFTERWARD

The reawakening of religious fervor that Teresa set in motion in Spain spread soon after her death beyond Spain and across Christendom with profound results for the Catholic Reformation. Because her country was then at the height of its power and wealth, what happened there tended to influence the course of the church.

Teresa is regarded as one of the outstanding women in the history of Spain, and her books on the mystical life are valued as gems of Spanish literature as well as treasuries of spirituality.

Her spiritual friendship with John of the Cross is perhaps her most famous relationship, but she had a great capacity for friendship with both men and women. Her circle of admirers ever widened the older she got.

Because women in Spain were so constricted by cultural norms, it is all the more remarkable how much she accomplished. (To be a woman at all, Teresa once remarked, was to feel your wings droop.)

A papal nuncio who referred to her as a "restless gadabout" complained, "She is ambitious and teaches theology as though she were a Doctor of the Church."[9] Teresa had the last word—not surprisingly—for she became the first woman in the church so designated. The honor came on September 27, 1970 (one week before Catherine of Siena was so named).

O SACRED HEART OF JESUS,

LUKEWARMNESS IN PRAYER
WAS TERESA'S COMPLAINT.
TO OVERCOME IT, SHE STRUGGLED,
YEARS IN THE DOING.
THAT PERSEVERANCE GAVE US A SAINT.

HEARTFELT PRAYER IS AVAILABLE
TO ANY OF US.
I ASK MYSELF:
CAN I SPARE THE TIME?
AMEN.

THE SEVENTEENTH CENTURY

LOUISE DE MARILLAC

BACKGROUND

France was on its way to supplanting Spain as the dominant power in Europe. Cardinal Richelieu, the king's chief minister of state, pushed the advance through political and economic means. In France the Catholic Reformation had gotten off to a slow start because of the turmoil connected with intermittent religious wars on its soil, while elsewhere on the continent, Protestants and Catholics engaged in battles too. At one point, to keep Catholic Austria from becoming too powerful, Cardinal Richelieu arranged for the French to join forces with Protestant Sweden in a move against Austria.

In the meantime, reforms instituted by the Council of Trent in the mid-sixteenth century had effected a sweeping house-cleaning of abuses, and in the process turned the church strongly in the direction of conservatism, not to reverse itself until Vatican II.

Women in religious life were more restricted in their activities than ever. In seventeenth-century France, though, women of the laity, particularly those of the upper classes, tended to have more educational opportunities and the chance to shine as individuals in society than they did in most European countries. From their ranks came some of the great names of contributors to the new spiritual vigor marking this period. Among them were individuals who aimed to live a Christian life in the world, although joining the Carmelites or other austere orders was also a popular choice. The first houses of reformed Carmelites had been set up in France in 1604, initially directed by nuns from Spain. Their contemplative spirituality had a significant influence on the French.

PARIS, FRANCE, JANUARY 1638

When Vincent de Paul learns from his friend Louise about the conditions at La Couche, he calls it "the shame of Paris."

Each year hundreds of babies born out of wedlock are being abandoned on church doorsteps and other public places by mothers too poor to keep them. State care is provided through a home called La Couche, operated by an appointed matron who is aided by two hired servants. To quiet the crying infants, the women administer laudanum (an opium preparation). Some babies are sold to practitioners of black magic and devil worship and used as ritual victims. Others are bought by professional beggars who break the babies' bones before employing them as props to arouse pity as the beggars ply their trade.

Something must be done to remedy this horror, Monsieur Vincent declares. Agreeing wholeheartedly, Louise begins, as she does with every undertaking, by drawing up guidelines. Experience tells her that building the right organization is the most critical phase.

17 : LOUISE DE MARILLAC

Initially, arrangements are made in 1638 to remove twelve infants from the infamous La Couche to be cared for instead by staff from her own community of young women devoted to helping the poor. In addition, she employs wet nurses; a mother herself, Louise knows the importance of breastfeeding, particularly for babies whose start in life has been so precarious. This model project grows so that within five years more than twelve hundred infants will have been cared for.

Of all the varied ministries Louise engages in, the ones associated with the welfare of children remain closest to her heart. Surely the loneliness she experienced as a child has something to do with it.

Her father, Louis de Marillac, was of distinguished family, and two of his brothers held high positions at the royal court. She was born during the period between her father's two marriages and never knew who her mother was. Her father acknowledged her as his natural daughter, providing for her upbringing, but she was never part of the family when he entered into a second, quite unhappy marriage with a widow who had four children.

At an early age she was placed in the care of an aunt who was a nun at a prestigious Dominican convent, and there the girl received an excellent classical education. She was thirteen when her father died. It was a great blow to her. After that her education took a more practical turn, for she boarded with a woman who taught her sewing, cooking and household management. Eager at the time to enter a religious order, Louise was turned down because of delicate health. That left only one alternative—marriage. Thus came about her union with Antoine le Gras, secretary to the Queen Regent, Marie de Medici.

When the marriage banns were proclaimed, Louise's status at birth became public knowledge—certainly a humiliation for her, since her husband's position entailed socializing with the nobility. The marriage, nevertheless, proved a happy one, and the birth of a son within a year was an occasion for rejoicing.

Along with her household and social obligations, Louise managed to fit in charitable work for her parish church. Despite this full life, she became at times quite introspective about her early desire to be a nun, feeling guilty that she had not been able to follow through. Spiritual directors advised her not to think about it. These episodes of melancholy may have been triggered by the strain of nursing her husband, whose health was on the wane.

After a prolonged illness, Antoine died in 1625, leaving Louise, at age thirty-four, with their twelve-year-old son Michel. Though Antoine had made provisions to insure her an income, still she had to adjust to one reduced in scale.

She moved to a smaller house on the Rue Saint-Victor, near Notre Dame, because that is the district where Michel went to school and where her spiritual director for the past year or two, Vincent de Paul, headquartered his company of mission priests. ("Monsieur" Vincent—as priests were addressed then—had not been eager to act as her director, yet gave in to pressure from a bishop friend. Louise, incidentally, was known as "Mademoiselle" le Gras. In seventeenth-century France only ladies of the high nobility were addressed as "Madame." After her husband's death, she resumed her maiden name, as was customary in France when the husband was of inferior rank.)

Louise continued her parish work of serving the poor, for she believed love of God is best shown in love of neighbor. She longed to make a more permanent kind of commitment, but Monsieur Vincent put her off. He characteristically waited until God's will was clear to him before taking any action.

In early May, 1629, her prayer was answered at last. Vincent sent a note explaining that he had been asked to give a mission outside of Paris and must leave at once, adding that there was work for her, too, at this place called Montmirail if she finds the idea agreeable. "Does your heart tell you to come there, Mademoiselle?"[1] Vincent wrote. Knowing very well what her response would be, he added instructions on which coach to take.

Louise's assignment in Montmirail was to spend some time reviewing the local "Charity." This was a volunteer group comprised of laypersons, primarily women, who served the sick and poor of their parish. Vincent had started the first such Charity when he was briefly a pastor in a rural parish more than twenty years before. (He was of peasant background himself.) After founding his order, the Congregation of the Mission, dedicated to preaching as well as works of mercy in Paris and elsewhere, he and his priests continued the practice of setting up local lay confraternities to attend to needs on a permanent basis. With the passage of time, some Charities lost their fervor, and others needed to be taught newer methods of dealing with problems related to poverty.

After Louise met with unqualified success in reinvigorating the Montmirail group, Vincent came to rely on her for visitations to other Charities. A delicate constitution did not hinder her from arduous journeys on public stage coaches. She stayed at the cheapest inns, for she wanted to be one with the poor. Her baggage was filled chiefly with medical supplies for parish confraternities. (Years of nursing her husband had given Louise a considerable knowledge of medicine.)

On arriving in a country parish she would impress the lay volunteers by her manner of instructing them through example, not just words, as this clearly cultured woman went into the rude hovels typical of the village poor to clean, cook and tend the sick.

On one of the early visitations Louise became acquainted with a cowherd, seventeen-year-old Marguerite Naseau, who was so determined to learn that she had taught herself to read. Then, in an eagerness to share, she had begun teaching others. This struck a responsive chord, for Louise, too, sought to promote education, especially for girls, seeing it as a way of overcoming their lack of opportunity. When she talked with Vincent about Marguerite's desire to come to Paris and work among the poor, they concluded that the vocation was a true one. Marguerite thus became the first young woman of peasant stock to lodge in Louise's home. More would follow.

Louise's "Little Company" evolved at just the right moment. For, though Vincent had established parish charities in Paris, many of the women with the luxury of time to volunteer came from aristocratic backgrounds. They consequently knew scarcely anything about performing the menial domestic chores necessary in caring for the sick poor. And even among those willing to try, many had husbands understandably alarmed about their wives going into the often vermin-infested houses of the poor.

Women from the villages, on the other hand, were accustomed to hard labor in addition to being free of the social strictures that go with an upper-class standing. (When some of the latter sent their servants to do the work for them, Vincent and Louise objected, since the whole point was to give of themselves.)

At the prompting of a close friend of Louise, a number of the highborn banded into a citywide association called Ladies of Charity, serving the poor directly when their husbands permitted and providing financial support for works of mercy. But the work itself fell increasingly on the shoulders of Louise's Little Company.

When she wanted to formalize her group—never having given up wanting to be a nun—Vincent resisted. He had seen what happened when his friend Bishop Francis de Sales cofounded with Jeanne de Chantal the Order of Visitation, intending that the sisters serve the world. The church decreed that congregations of women must be cloistered, and the Visitation nuns unhappily took that state. In another instance an Englishwoman named Mary Ward had attempted to obtain papal approval for her Institute of the Blessed Virgin Mary comprised of teaching nuns— an apostolate "in the world"—but church authorities insisted they conduct their ministry within the confines of the cloister. When Mary Ward was unable to accept that, her Institute was suppressed in 1631.

Vincent and Louise agree that the Daughters of Charity *must* be free to serve. As he so memorably tells the members of Louise's Little Company: "Your convent...will be the house of the sick; your cell, a hired room; your chapel, the parish church; your cloister, the streets of the city or the wards of the hospital; your enclosure, obedience; your grating, the fear of God; your veil, holy modesty."[2]

A solution was in the making. On November 29, 1633, a red-letter day for Louise, four young women agree to live a common life in her home as laypersons, not nuns. Some months later, with eleven under her direction, Louise presents them with a rule of life she had worked out; it stresses at least an hour each day for prayer. To impress upon them the way in which they ought to view their vocation, Louise will often quote to them words that God had spoken to Catherine of Siena, as recorded in Catherine's *Dialogue.* "A soul who truly loves Me also loves his neighbor, since love for Me and love of the neighbor are one and the same. Your love for your neighbor is the measure of your love for Me.... The soul who loves My truth never wearies of devoting himself to the service of others."[3]

(The problem of vows will eventually be circumvented when Vincent arranges for the Daughters of Charity to renew their promises on an annual basis rather than taking permanent vows as traditional orders do. This will seem to satisfy ecclesiastical authorities, who consequently see the women as of a lesser status, not true religious.)

Although, in the early years, theirs is not officially a religious congregation, the public regards the women as nuns. They wear ordinary dress—modest gray gowns and white kerchief head coverings—but are easily identifiable by their uniform attire. (The distinctive headdress known as the cornette came later.) People react with shock at the idea of nuns freely going about city streets to work among the poor. When her Daughters are subject to taunts and sometimes stone-throwing, Louise, while sympathetic, advises patience, assuring them that this would pass.

Aided by her guidelines—abetted by her organizational ability—the Daughters soon earn respect for a range of ministries. They bring, for instance, a progressive approach to nursing at Hotel Dieu, the mammoth hospital of Paris. So little does the hired staff know about even elementary hygiene that a mother with a new baby may be placed next to a patient with smallpox; the overcrowding is such that at times a bed meant for two ends up with six occupants. The Daughters' reputation for competence results in their being the first women sent to the battlefield to nurse wounded soldiers at Sedan in 1641.

France's involvement in the Thirty Years' War (1618–1648) and civil war, too, makes for unsettled conditions. An estimated forty thousand beggars roam the streets of Paris. At three sites in the city, Louise and her sisters coordinate soup kitchens, serving eight thousand meals daily. War refugees must be cared for, and free schools teaching occupational skills opened for poor girls in both the war-torn provinces and Paris. Louise develops as a pilot project the first hospice for the elderly, providing workrooms where they can feel useful by employing their talents to make saleable items. The commissions give them pocket money, which the men tend to spend on wine.

Vincent asks Louise to train some of her Daughters for nursing work in the prisons, where conditions reduce many of the convicts to the level of beasts. Confident of her ability to meet the challenge, he turns over the project to what he regards as her "adventurous mind." Though not naïve about the possibilities of danger, she instructs the sisters to pray and behave with modesty and God will keep them from harm. No harm befalls any of them.

Louise still finds time to worry about her son Michel, who lacks the capabilities she likes to think he possesses. Vincent will often chide her about being overly anxious about her son's welfare, though admittedly Michel takes his time in finally settling on an occupation (with Vincent's help) and marriage. He then goes on to lead a contented life.

Vincent, in turn, fusses over Louise's welfare, giving her such homey advice as "eat eggs" when she is ill and insisting she not fast during Lent since she needs her strength for her social work.

He leans on her too, for theirs is a relationship of mutuality. On one occasion he confesses, "God alone knows, Mademoiselle, what He has done for me in giving you to me. In heaven you will know."[4] Their exchange of notes and letters when apart provides history with a wealth of information.

These two noble hearts, after long lives of service, pass from this earth within six months of each other.

AFTERWARD

The Daughters of Charity was the first community of women since the early church who, from its inception, did not live a cloistered or contemplative life and remained free from then on to minister to the poor and sick as Louise and Vincent had envisioned. Louise liked to say she contemplated Christ in the poor.

She drew her original vocations from among peasant women who would otherwise have gone into domestic service or become farm laborers. In the process she and Vincent created a revolutionary form of religious community, unleashing a power latent in women to overwhelm the world with monumental good works. At the time of her death in 1660, there were already more than forty houses of her sisters. Today the Daughters of Charity serve on five continents.

In almost as radical a move, Vincent had her conduct retreats (women did not do this) for ladies of nobility while he did so for the men, saying that they needed spiritual nourishment as much as the poor needed their soup kitchens.

Louise and Vincent together pioneered in all aspects of social service. Space limits describing all their "firsts." They of course paved the way for all the other congregations who engage in social work and teaching.

HOLY SPIRIT,

IN HER LIFE'S WORK,
LOUISE PROCEEDED
ONE STEP AT A TIME,
NEVER DREAMING TO BE BLESSED
WITH DAUGHTERS NUMBERING LIKE THE STARS.

MAY I DO THE GOOD
THAT I CAN,
LEAVING THE FUTURE
IN GOD'S CAPABLE HANDS.
AMEN.

THE EIGHTEENTH CENTURY

ANNE MARIE JAVOUHEY

BACKGROUND

An intellectual revolution paved the way for the French Revolution—much of it carried on in cosmopolitan salons presided over by aristocratic Frenchwomen of eighteenth-century Paris. Long before, however, the Renaissance that exalted human accomplishments had initiated the movement toward the modern, secular age. The Renaissance was followed by revolt against an authoritarian church at Rome. Then the exploration of new lands around the globe opened European minds to wider horizons. Finally, the Age of Enlightenment, centered in eighteenth-century France, extolled human reason to the extent that it became a god in place of God. Institutional religion was downgraded when not ignored outright by the intellectuals.

During Louis XIV's seventy-year reign (ending in 1715), France came to be Europe's wealthiest country—and undoubtedly its most extravagant. There was a steady drain on the state treasury to pay for French involvement in a succession of wars (including financial support for the American Revolution), in addition to the high cost of the luxury-loving royal court at Versailles. This made necessary a crushing burden of taxation levied on the lower classes while the nobility and higher clergy escaped taxation.

People's attitude toward parish priests was usually benign, for the lower clergy were often as impoverished as the peasants to whom they ministered. But the resentment the poor directed at the nobility and the higher clergy grew stronger. The situation could not continue. With an angry mob's storming of the Bastille in 1789, the traditional social and political order broke down completely.

VILLAGE OF CHAMBLANC, FRANCE, 1797

Hearing shouts and pounding on the front door after dark, the Javouhey family and their guest—an outlawed priest—are paralyzed by fear. All but seventeen-year-old Nanette; she urges the priest to duck into the closet, then coolly opens the front door to greet four men. One is the local deputy for the revolutionary government, who demands to know where the priest is.

Nanette laughs as she denies they are harboring a priest. She asks for their coats and moves to hang them in the closet, meanwhile reminding her father he should get their company a glass of wine. The men decline the offer, retrieve their coats and go on their way, anxious to track down the fugitive priest they are sure is hiding somewhere in the neighborhood. If caught, he'll likely be executed.

This is only one of a number of times that Nanette keeps her head—while risking her life—to safeguard a priest. When the revolution in France had begun almost a decade before, its leaders waged war against the church in violent reaction to the years in which many in the hierarchy lived in luxury, associating with the nobility, while the majority of the people as well as the lower clergy suffered poverty. Church lands were confiscated and religious institutions closed. Priests who refused to take a civil oath—which, in effect, would make them a part of the civil service—were treated as criminals. When the Reign of Terror broke out in 1793, thousands of priests and nuns went to the guillotine or were condemned to prisons in the South American colony of French Guiana, such as the infamous Devil's Island. Priests who escaped capture but did not flee abroad joined an underground network to serve devout Catholics who were forced to practice their faith secretly—like those in the village where Nanette and her family lived.

Growing up in these times so terrifying for religious people, Nanette wants still to be a nun. She creates a sanctuary in a corner of the garden for daily prayer and, despite her youth, teaches the forbidden catechism to the children of Chamblanc under cover of her father's barn.

Even if convents were open to postulants, Balthazar Javouhey would object. He wants his favorite daughter to marry a farmer and settle down to a normal life. Their disagreement over her future reaches the stage in which, at times, she sends him letters via a younger sister rather than argue face-to-face. Nanette keeps hoping the political situation will change. And with Napoleon's takeover of the government in 1801, the church's fortunes do improve markedly. Napoleon makes peace with the pope and allows the reopening of religious houses. It is a wise move, for the country needs all the help possible to repair the havoc wrought by the revolution. No institution can equal the church for making human resources available for education and social services.

In this welcome new freedom, Nanette goes away to convents for two brief periods, but neither one seems the right place for her despite the strong attraction she has to the vocation itself.

Her mother Claudine, a woman of great piety, seems only to shrug when her husband gets riled. While Balthazar does not understand Nanette and wishes fervently that she would come to her senses, he unfailingly supports her endeavors—as when, after her first convent experience, Nanette seeks to open a school in a neighboring village. In less than a year she returns home in failure. The next venture in a village thirty miles away also ends in failure. Financial assistance promised by village priests does not materialize owing to their own poverty. Lacking help with the work and without funds, she must go back to her family again.

The priest advising her suggests a Trappistine convent for training in spiritual practices to serve as her bulwark. After Nanette spends a few tranquil months there, he counsels that she must again resume the active life.

Her third attempt at trying to run a school for orphans proves the most disastrous experiment of all. At one point food for the children entrusted to her runs out. A woebegone Nanette goes to pray at a nearby chapel. Knocking on the tabernacle door, she cries, "I need help.... Please, please help." In answer, a voice says, "Have you no faith in me?"[1] Then it tells her to return to the orphanage. She runs back to see her father and brother Pierre just arriving in a cart loaded with food.

Nevertheless, this proves but a stopgap measure, and she must return to Chamblanc where her father—throwing up his hands in despair—boards off half the family home as a convent. For it seems that Nanette's three younger sisters want to be nuns too, teaching nuns.

Balthazar builds a small schoolhouse on his property. He also transports back to Chamblanc the orphans from the last failed school to become the first pupils in this new enterprise. When neighbors ask who the youngsters arriving in his cart are,

Balthazar proudly replies, "These are my daughter's children."[2]

When Pope Pius VII, on a tour through France, schedules a visit to the town of Chalon, seventy-five miles from her home, Nanette decides to join the welcoming throngs. She finds herself granted a few minutes to speak with the pope, and when she tells him of her work in teaching the faith, he warmly approves. This spurs her to accept an offer to run a parish school in Chalon. Seeing the excellent results achieved by the young woman, the pastor encourages her to think of starting her own congregation.

Good fortune continues to shine for the moment on Nanette, as the government makes available an unused seminary outside of Chalon with facilities to accommodate 125 students. Here she and the eight now on her teaching staff, including her three sisters, model their life on that of a religious community. The schools at Chamblanc and Chalon still operate under their auspices. Nanette takes to signing her letters home as "Sister Anne Marie." (Anne Marie was her baptismal name; Nanette is the family's pet name for her.)

At age twenty-seven she officially becomes Sister Anne Marie, for her congregation, with herself as superior, gets approval from the requisite episcopal and government authorities. The small band of teaching sisters intends to conduct schools and orphanages, with emphasis on educating the poor. There are plans also to aid the sick and aged.

Several years later the government reclaims the seminary, saying the group was granted its use only temporarily. Once more Balthazar Javouhey comes to the rescue in 1812, buying the little community both house and property at Cluny, a place rich in history as the center of church reform in the Middle Ages. Henceforth, the congregation will call itself the Sisters of St. Joseph of Cluny. This puts the motherhouse in the diocese of Autun, therefore coming under obedience to its bishop, a circumstance that will cause no end of trouble in Anne Marie's future. But for the moment she is concerned with the congregation's rapid expansion. With a flood of applicants, new convents must be set up.

Part of the expansion includes opening a school in Paris where Anne Marie inaugurates a controversial but highly successful system of education. Known as the Lancaster system after its developer, English educator Joseph Lancaster, it makes use of the older, brighter students in a school as teaching assistants. This enables a limited professional staff to teach larger numbers with greater effectiveness. The method soon proves a boon to mass education for the poor. A major point of controversy is the system's origin in England, a traditional enemy of France.

Anne Marie consequently enjoys a reputation as one of the country's leading educators, drawing attention and a visit from the governor of a French colony in the Indian Ocean off the eastern coast of Africa. He asks for teaching nuns, and when Anne Marie discovers that most of the children in the colony of Bourbon (known today as Reunion) are black, there is no question that she will dispatch sisters to implement her new system of education. Years before, though she was not then aware of people whose color was other than white, she had a vision of many dark-skinned boys and girls, along with a woman who identified herself as Teresa of Avila and said, "These are the children that God has given you. He wishes you to form a new congregation to take care of them."[3] The vision had occurred at a time when Anne Marie was praying to know God's will for her life.

She longs to go with the four sisters assigned to the island of Bourbon, but her first consideration must be to figure out ways of financing the new schools that the congregation is opening throughout France.

The work at Bourbon, meanwhile, progresses exceedingly well. Government authorities are so pleased that they request Sisters of St. Joseph for colonies in the West Indies, South America and Senegal. The latter, on Africa's west coast, is France's oldest and most neglected colony.

Anne Marie appoints her youngest sister, Rosalie, to be in charge of a small group of nuns at the Senegal mission. Once settled there, Rosalie writes back: "Were I to describe to you what I have witnessed and learned of the habits and customs of this savage country you would not read my account of it a second time, but rather close your eyes to it and pray that God in His mercy would enlighten the darkness and ignorance of these unhappy people. It will take years to train them, but our Sisters are indefatigable."[4] As culturally insensitive as Rosalie's remarks are, she reflects the general thinking of her day among missionaries. Anne Marie will pursue a different course.

Anne Marie feels compelled to see for herself. At first opportunity, with affairs running smoothly in France, she impulsively sets off for the colony early in 1822 to spend several years as a missionary. Like the other nuns, she will nurse rather than teach, for that is the critical need in Senegal. Anne Marie also encounters the problem of slavery. Seeing a ten-year-old girl about to be consigned to service, she buys the girl for three hundred francs, and Florence is from then on her steady companion.

When Anne Marie at last returns to France with Florence in tow, she is heartsick to learn the extent of troubles fomented by one of her own nuns in the Bourbon colony. A Sister Thais, looking to take over as superior there in every respect even though Anne Marie had named someone else to the post, has manipulated the officials and priests in the colony and even the nuns, so that all believe she is but a meek and pious nun being much abused by congregation headquarters in France. Because of the

distances involved (a ship's journey, carrying mail or replacement nuns, takes up to six months), it requires several years'
effort to untangle Sister Thais's web of deceit. Anne Marie is
finally obliged to work through friends at the royal court before
the government ministry with the final say on the colonies orders
Thais and her band of rebel sisters back to France. None, of
course, remains with the Cluny congregation.

When the government requests teachers and nurses for the
South American colony of Guiana, Anne Marie at age fifty leads
the contingent from Cluny. While so far from home, she learns of
her father's death. Balthazar, ever supportive, had been looking
after her brother Pierre's wife and children so that Pierre could
lend aid to Anne Marie in bringing order to the new mission. In
the period before she left for Guiana, her mother had died, as
well as Anne Marie's adopted daughter Florence, whose health
had failed under the strain of the adjustment from African to
French climate.

When Anne Marie has black children attend school alongside
the French children in Guiana, her popularity with the French
settlers plummets. In fact, they resist any attempts she makes to
improve the lot of the natives.

After five years in the colony, she returns to Paris, where a
government commission has requested her help in organizing a
model project for freed slaves in Guiana. The government has
passed a bill to free them after a seven-year probationary period
in which slaves are expected to prove themselves capable of being
self-sufficient. Details to implement the bill need to be worked
out. Though ready to assume charge of the project, Anne Marie
must first deal with trouble in her own backyard again.

This time it comes from the new bishop of the Autun diocese
where the Cluny motherhouse is located. Bishop d'Hericourt is
of the old school, determined to assert his episcopal authority

over the woman he regards as an upstart. It marks the beginning of an eighteen-year war between the two, with the bishop using every means at his disposal (including high-placed friends in the church) to make life difficult for her. At one point he even accuses the Cluny nuns of wearing an "indecent" guimpe (the white collar rimming their blue habits). D'Hericourt threatens to withhold the permission she needs in order to leave the diocese for the mission in South America. Thus she is forced to sign an agreement granting him the final say in running her order.

Finally able to leave for French Guiana, she stops long enough in Senegal to pick up sixty African women who are in the market for husbands. (Most of the six hundred slaves she will be working with are male.) Once in Guiana she organizes a settlement in a district called Mana to initiate her project. Despite opposition from colonial plantation owners, who see their free labor lost forever and economic competition besides, Mana flourishes. Having grown up a farm girl, Anne Marie knows the skills necessary to survive in an agricultural community. But part of the success is owed to her guidance in setting up a distillery, using the abundant sugarcane raised to produce rum for an eager French market.

Ignoring—and sometimes escaping—threats to her life, Anne Marie further wins the favor of her slaves-on-probation when she walks fifty miles through jungle to report the murder of one to the colonial administration. A plantation owner trying to reclaim his former slaves from Mana had burned one of them alive.

Although thousands of miles away, Bishop d'Hericourt gets back into the picture by allying himself with the plantation owners. He also has the local bishop excommunicate Anne Marie because she refuses to sign another document sent from Autun, this one allowing d'Hericourt to remake the Cluny constitution. Being deprived of the Eucharist causes her enormous spiritual suffering. She carries on, nevertheless, with her government assignment, departing Mana only when the slaves have proved self-sufficiency and are assured their freedom. When the Mana colony receives the vote, they want Anne Marie as their delegate to the French parliament and are disappointed that she cannot be. She tells others that Mana has been the place of her greatest happiness.

In Paris again Anne Marie is able to find a friendly bishop who reinstates her in the good graces of the church. D'Hericourt still continues to interfere with Cluny, but the Revolution of 1848 prevents her from going to Rome to appeal. During the brief but violent revolution the archbishop of Paris, who has been backing d'Hericourt, is killed while trying to cross a barricade in the city. (Just the night before Anne Marie, recognized by a guard manning the same barricade, was allowed to pass through without question.) A new archbishop arranges for the motherhouse to be moved to Paris permanently—out of d'Hericourt's reach. Having already won freedom for the slaves, Anne Marie wins freedom for her congregation, too.

AFTERWARD

At her death two years later, at age seventy-one, Anne Marie's order had 118 houses, with seven hundred sisters in France and three hundred more in Africa, South America, India and Tahiti.

In testimony to her accomplishments a government proclamation was issued in praise of Sister Anne Marie. King Louis Philippe (with whom she was in great favor) once said to friends, "Take my word for it. Madame Javouhey is a great man!"[5]

In the nineteenth-century church France was to take the leading role in supplying missionaries to work with people of color in the Third World. The same year that Anne Marie embarked on her first missionary journey to Senegal, 1822, Pauline Jaricot, a twenty-three-year-old woman in Lyons, France, was organizing the missionary aid society that was destined to grow into the Society for the Propagation of the Faith.

Years ahead of her time, Anne Marie became more and more convinced of the need for a native clergy, but others did not support the idea. (In 1950 Anne Marie was beatified.)

Her congregation today remains international in scope, with many convents throughout the world. It engages in all kinds of work, depending on the needs of the particular area: teaching, pastoral ministry in parishes and in hospitals, religious education, nursing, rural ministry.

LORD GOD,

AHEAD OF HER TIME,
ANNE MARIE OPENED DOORS
IN WAYS THAT RAISED HACKLES,
BUT ALSO RAISED HOPE
FOR THOSE WISHING IT MOST.

LONGING TO OPEN DOORS, TOO,
I LOOK AROUND.
WHO IN MY WORLD NEEDS HELP?
SHALL I BE THE FIRST TO VOLUNTEER?
AMEN.

THE NINETEENTH CENTURY

ELIZABETH LANGE

BACKGROUND

Maryland became a colony in 1634 under the aegis of an English-born Catholic, Lord Baltimore. Freedom was guaranteed for all religions, making Maryland attractive to Protestant settlers as well as Catholics; they soon outnumbered the Catholic population. After that Catholics were relegated to second-class status and not even allowed to vote until after the Revolutionary War, when they proved their patriotism to the satisfaction of Protestant Americans (at least for the moment).

In 1784 a priest named John Carroll (cousin to Charles Carroll, a signer of the Declaration of Independence) was appointed by the Vatican as "Superior of the Mission in the thirteen United States." (Before that the overseer was in London.) A few years later Carroll became bishop of Baltimore. The original diocese extended north to Maine, south to Georgia and west to the Mississippi River. Catholics in this territory numbered about thirty-five thousand; the bulk of them lived in Maryland and Pennsylvania. In all the United States at this time less than 10 percent of the population professed membership in any denomination.

The Baltimore see was soon divided into smaller dioceses and additional bishops named. John Carroll himself had the distinction of being elected bishop by the Maryland clergy as their candidate, following a request the priests sent to Rome. The pope had expected two or three names to be submitted, but Carroll was the overwhelming choice, receiving twenty-four out of twenty-five votes. The pope subsequently gave his approval. Some priests had also proposed that Mass be said in English, but whether that ever actually took place remains uncertain.

Maryland was a natural hub of American Catholic life. One of the first seminaries was opened in Baltimore just prior to the nineteenth century. Shortly afterward the first parochial school was established in Emmitsburg, Maryland, by Elizabeth Seton, who also founded the first American religious order of nuns.

Black Catholics, however, need not apply for seminary, school or convent. In fact, religious orders as well as individual Catholic laypeople continued to own slaves, and the church never did play a significant role in the later campaign to free them.

BALTIMORE, MARYLAND, OCTOBER 1847

On his knees the young priest begs the archbishop, "Most Reverend Father, only give me your blessing, with your permission on trial."[1]

Until now Archbishop Eccleston has seen no point in providing support—moral or financial—for the Oblate Sisters of Providence. In fact, in the past he has suggested that the congregation disband, and his opinion is also shared by many in the

Catholic community, both clergy and laity. But when Father Thaddeus Anwander, a Redemptorist priest from Germany, learned of the nuns' desperate situation, he told his superior, who then sent him to the archbishop.

Anwander hopes to be assigned the pastoral care of the sisters, but first Archbishop Eccleston must approve it. The humility with which the priest pleads his case wins over the archbishop, and that same day Father Anwander hurries to the Oblate house to give the nuns the good news. He promises them the kind of help that got the order started.

The story actually begins about thirty years before with the arrival in Baltimore of Elizabeth Lange, a refugee born in Cuba of San Domingan parents. (Her father may have been white; her mother was black. In any case, Elizabeth is considered "colored.") The Maryland city had earlier become a haven for French Catholics fleeing revolution in their country. The upheaval, felt as far away as France's colonies in the Caribbean, precipitated another wave of refugees, attracted to Baltimore by the existence of a large French-speaking community.

Haven notwithstanding, Maryland is also a slaveholding state where harsh discrimination against people of color is common and education for blacks almost nonexistent. Disturbed by what she encounters, Elizabeth, who is well-educated herself, feels called to do what she can.

She has a small income, possibly from her father in Cuba. (Shy and reserved, Elizabeth will say little of her life previous to the Baltimore period.) With the aid of another refugee, Marie Balas, she organizes a free school for black children in her home.

Ministry to San Domingan Catholics—both white and black—has become a special province of Sulpician priests, in addition to their operation of St. Mary's Seminary in Baltimore. (Sulpicians were also refugees of French background.) At the

19 : ELIZABETH LANGE

seminary chapel, which also serves as a parish church, as a matter of religious protocol, seminarians and male religious worship in the Upper Chapel, while the French-speaking parishioners, white and black, use the Lower Chapel, or *Chapelle Basse*. (It is not clear whether whites and blacks worship at the same time.)

When Father James Joubert is named chaplain for the black congregation, he discovers that many of the children in his catechism class cannot read the lessons. While outlining a plan to open a school for them, he learns that Elizabeth and several other women in the congregation have been running a small free school at home for ten years, but because of insufficient funds it is in danger of being discontinued.

Joubert meets Elizabeth, and they discuss the possibility of working together. Impressed with the commitment she shows to her faith, he promises his backing if she will form a religious community of black women to provide a teaching base, for, at that time, no order allowed blacks to enter. As part of the arrangement Joubert is expected to keep the accounts, and Elizabeth will regulate community life and oversee instruction.

Joubert is successful in acquiring funds from several affluent whites originally from San Domingo. Subsequently, a house is rented—large enough to accommodate eleven boarders and nine day students paying tuition, along with four orphan girls admitted free.

Father Joubert approaches the new Archbishop Whitfield to gain approval for the initial phase of Elizabeth Lange's religious community. (She has quickly found three others willing to join.) The man Whitfield just replaced had voiced some objections but, to Joubert's relief, the new archbishop warmly welcomes the proposal.

The four aspiring nuns move into the schoolhouse to begin their year's novitiate while also teaching. Before the year is over their landlord gives notice, saying he has other plans for the property. A bit of difficulty is encountered in renting another place the moment an owner discovers the prospective tenants' color. But eventually a white doctor of San Domingan origin comes to their aid and makes a house available at affordable cost.

On July 2, 1829, the women pronounce vows—the first black women ever formed into their own religious community. According to their Rule: "The Oblate Sisters of Providence are a Religious Society of virgins and widows of color. Their end is to consecrate themselves to God in a special manner not only to sanctify themselves and thereby secure the glory of God, but also to work for the Christian education of colored children."[2] Elizabeth Lange takes the name Sister Mary.

They adopt a habit consisting of a black dress, cape and bonnet. (Indoors, the bonnet is replaced by a white cap banded with a black ribbon.) In his diary Father Joubert tells of the women's feelings of discouragement over public reaction to black women in habits. Nuns in general were quite accustomed to being pelted with mud or stones as well as subjected to verbal insults, for America's Catholic minority was often discriminated against. But Elizabeth Lange, now Sister Mary, and her companions also have to endure the same treatment from white Catholics. Joubert admits to his diary of hearing from white parishioners who "could not think of the idea of seeing these poor girls (colored girls) wearing the religious habit and constituting a religious community."[3] He must even contend with some members of the clergy who maintain that blacks have neither souls to be saved nor minds capable of being taught.

He presents the situation to the archbishop, who replies, "[Monsieur] Joubert, it is not lightly but with reflection that I approved your project. I knew and saw the finger of God....

Besides, have I not the power to make foundations in my diocese, in my episcopal city, of any religious establishment whatever?"[4]

That settled, the archbishop promises to protect the new foundation. Joubert relays his message to the nuns. Thus bolstered, they persevere. Sister Mary would later say of Joubert: "He was the greatest friend the Oblates ever had."[5]

About herself she speaks little, though community annals note of this petite yet physically strong—and strong-willed—woman: "If there was work to be done, she was the first to volunteer."[6]

When a cholera epidemic strikes the city in 1832, Sister Mary is among the four Oblates who spend a month caring for patients in the city's almshouse, staying until the worst is over. In the appeal for help, the Baltimore Bureau of the Poor had originally asked the Sisters of Charity (the congregation founded by Elizabeth Seton) for eight nuns. That order was able to spare only half the number, so the Oblates stepped in. (All eleven sisters—for the order had grown—offered to serve. The Baltimore City Council later issued a resolution publicly thanking the Sisters of Charity but making no mention of the Oblates.)

The order suffers its first loss because of the epidemic. The nun who had earlier nursed the archbishop back to health after his bout with cholera succumbs to the disease herself while caring for Whitfield's stricken housekeeper. Burial is in the Cathedral cemetery, in the section set apart for the colored.

When the epidemic subsides, the nuns resume their teaching duties. The only blight on their days comes from continuing complaints by white neighbors of their presence. But this is offset by Whitfield's unflagging support, along with the happiness engendered by Rome's approval of their congregation.

Because their residence is some distance from St. Mary's Seminary, the archbishop gives permission for the Blessed

Sacrament to be reserved in the convent chapel. (The diary of one of the sisters says of Sister Mary: "The Blessed Sacrament was always her refuge."[7]) Father Joubert's diary makes note of a feast day Mass in the chapel served for the first time by two of the students, with a third carrying the censer: "These were girls."[8]

To obtain more pupils, the nuns place an advertisement in the 1835 *United States Catholic Almanac*, explaining that the Oblates offer "A School for Colored Girls." The school's prospectus, presumably prepared by Father Joubert, lists the subjects taught: reading, writing, French, English, arithmetic, all kinds of fine sewing, embroidery, beadwork and gold work, geography, music, washing and ironing (the last two, no doubt, because most students are expected to "become mothers of families or domestic servants"[9]).

Life at the school is close-knit for teachers and children, whether they are praying the rosary together at noon or sharing the midday meal. At the end of the school day, while the boarding students study or enjoy recreation, the nuns sew as an income-producing activity, including vestments for the seminary.

The community continues to grow in the number of both sisters and pupils. One other addition in 1836 is Sister Mary's elderly mother, who comes from Cuba after the death of her husband. He has left an estate amounting to $1,411.59, which is contributed to the Oblates. (Sister Mary had already donated the major part of her assets at the time the order was founded.)

The Oblates' relatively peaceful existence changes abruptly with the death of Father Joubert in 1843 and that of Archbishop Whitfield a year later. Many former supporters cease helping. Direct diocesan funding had never been available, though Whitfield's endorsement in the past encouraged some benefactors. When Joubert's superior at the seminary asks support for the Oblates' work from the new archbishop, Samuel Eccleston, the latter reportedly replied, "What good is it?"[10] He thinks the education of black children is unimportant and suggests the congregation be dissolved. From among the Baltimore clergy (even those the sisters believed were on their side) come suggestions that, for black women, being good domestics takes priority over being nuns.

The Sulpician Society decides that running the seminary is all it can handle at the moment, leaving no one to spare as chaplain for the Oblates. This means the nuns no longer have Mass in their chapel or an assigned confessor. Adding to the sadness of these days is the death of Sister Mary's close friend, Marie Balas, one of the original Oblates.

To earn rent money and to feed the children at the school, ten of whom are orphans boarding free, the women take in washing. Sister Mary, along with another nun, accepts employment in the seminary kitchen. In the face of so many difficulties, two other nuns depart the community.

It is at this point that the young Redemptorist, Father Anwander, arrives on the scene and offers to become their chaplain, begging the reluctant Archbishop Eccleston for the privilege. Proving his good intentions, Father Anwander goes from house to house in Baltimore, seeking to enroll more tuition-paying students from the black district as well as asking donations. For the community, which had dwindled to twelve sisters with no postulants or novices in sight and only twenty remaining students, a new period of growth ensues. With Redemptorist support, enrollment increases to one hundred day students and sixty boarders, and the number of sisters doubles. Another school is built to accommodate more than fifty boys.

In this pre–Civil War period bitter racial hatred is evidenced in one ugly incident. A national organization called the "Know-

Nothings" (who are virulently anti-Catholic as well as anti-black) batter down the convent door in a rage, though none of the sisters is injured.

Just about the time the war begins, Father Anwander, after thirteen years with them, must leave. Direction of the Oblates is assigned to the Jesuits, who have opened Loyola College near the convent. The new chaplain, Father Miller, sees them through some rough days during the war. When it is over, the nuns again need additional space to take in black children orphaned by the conflict. In 1866 the Jesuits purchase a house for them with the understanding that the sisters, in exchange, will do the college laundry.

Also that year, at the Second Plenary Council of Baltimore, American bishops plead with priests to consecrate themselves to "the service of the colored people."

At various times over the years Oblates attempt to open schools in other places, including other states, but the traditional problems persist: failure to receive diocesan funding anywhere, black parents too poor to pay tuition and white Catholics unwilling to donate.

When the Jesuit Father Miller suffers deteriorating health, a fourth order, the Josephites, is assigned to direct the nuns. The Josephites are also working in the city's first black parish.

Though it comes a little late, the aging Sister Mary lives long enough to see what the Oblates have dreamed of for years: a public display of support from the hierarchy, Catholics and civic authorities at the order's golden jubilee celebration in 1879.

As a final blessing Father Anwander—who never lost interest even after he was reassigned—just happens to visit when Sister Mary is on her deathbed. To her joy, he is there to give her the last rites (now known as anointing of the sick).

AFTERWARD

During Elizabeth Lange's lifetime, the black Oblates were not allowed admission to Catholic colleges. When they needed the special training necessary to teach accredited high school subjects, the women had to rely on clergy and religious from white colleges who were willing to come to the Oblate house and give instruction. The breakthrough came years later when Villanova in Pennsylvania became the first Catholic university to admit them to summer school in 1924. There were by then black Catholic colleges.

The Oblate Sisters of Providence today have missions in Baltimore, Buffalo and Miami as well as two missions in Costa Rica. They also have novitiate houses in Baltimore and Costa Rica. (Their mission in Cuba, begun around 1900, was terminated when Fidel Castro came to power.) Their primary concern remains education of the poor.

American nuns of the nineteenth century preserved the faith of the numerous immigrants who came as political or economic refugees. They did it by imbuing immigrant children with the tenets of Catholicism through the parochial school system pioneered early in the century by Elizabeth Seton.

Anti-Catholic feeling so powerful at the start of that century was considerably mitigated by the equally powerful example of nuns establishing schools which Protestant children might also attend in cities on the frontier and of nuns valiantly nursing victims in epidemics and on Civil War battlefields. In addition, the sisterhood organized and operated a multitude of social services wherever these were lacking.

The strength of the Catholic church in the United States is due more to nuns than any other single group, although—witness Elizabeth Lange—recognition has been long in coming.

In 1991 the cause for her sainthood began in the Archdiocese of Baltimore with a formal investigation into her life. In 2004 the requisite documentation was forwarded to the Sacred Congregation for the Causes of Saints in Rome. In an often lengthy process the candidate is considered, in order, for the title of venerable, blessed and, finally, saint. Elizabeth Lange could one day become the first woman of color in the United States to be canonized.

LORD JESUS CHRIST,

IN THE FACE OF OBSTACLES,
ONE AFTER THE OTHER,
SISTER MARY SHOWED QUIET STRENGTH.
SURELY IT CAME FROM THE EUCHARIST,
WHICH WAS HER REFUGE.

HOW BLESSED WE ARE
FOR THE GIFT OF EUCHARIST,
MEANT TO TRANSFORM US.
LET US UNWRAP THE GIFT!
AMEN.

19 : ELIZABETH LANGE

THE TWENTIETH CENTURY

JEAN DONOVAN

BACKGROUND

In 1908 the Catholic church in the United States ceased being classed as mission territory by the Vatican. In 1911 came the founding of the Catholic Foreign Mission Society (otherwise known as Maryknoll). A year later that order opened the first seminary in the country to train missionaries for work overseas. American sisters, brothers and priests would now take their turn at serving mission territories.

Not to be left out, the laity joined in the apostolate at home, providing social service based on the gospel through volunteer lay organizations. Dorothy Day and Peter Maurin's Catholic Worker movement and its Hospitality Houses, and Catherine de Hueck Doherty and Eddie Doherty's Friendship House in Harlem, for example, were both conceived in the 1930s. The

Legion of Mary, a lay movement international in scope begun in Dublin in 1921, found its way to the United States.

Vatican II (1962–1965) set in motion tremendous changes in the church. Encompassing both liturgy and a fresh spirit of openness, it called for looking at what it means to be church not only from a Western perspective. One region to feel the effects most profoundly was Latin America. The real watershed in the Latin church came in 1968 when its bishops met at Medellín, Colombia, and made a commitment to work for the rights of the poor and to end social injustice, giving impetus to the concept of "liberation theology." (Throughout its history, the Latin church had traditionally allied itself with the ruling class.)

Maryknoll had been active in the region for some time when in the mid-1970s it issued a call for help from the laity in the United States, a need prompted by the sharp drop-off in priestly and religious vocations. The laity responded. Many volunteered for the order's own lay missioner program; in some cases, local churches or dioceses took on projects abroad and availed themselves of Maryknoll's expertise in training missioners for the transcultural experience.

LA LIBERTAD, EL SALVADOR, AUGUST 1 0, 1 9 7 9

Arriving in this tropical Pacific Coast town, young Jean Donovan hears the tolling of church bells. She learns that they are being rung in tribute to a local priest who was gunned down at the altar of his church. Parishioners who witnessed the murder say it was committed by three they recognized as policemen.

For Jean, it can hardly be the most promising introduction to her new calling as a lay missioner in Latin America's smallest country. Despite a worsening of violence, the general feeling among North Americans volunteering in El Salvador seems to be that they are relatively safe. The native clergy and native church workers involved with the poor are objects of reprisal.

The situation originated a few years previously when priests began identifying with the poor and preaching the need for social justice. In the eyes of the entrenched powers, that was a revolutionary move inevitably leading to class struggle and Communism. (In the early 1970s the only Communists actually in operation were two small groups of urban guerrillas from middle-class backgrounds.)

Prosperous landowners who, along with the military, controlled the country felt their position threatened. Soon there were death squads aimed at eliminating "Communist" priests as well as other "subversives." Those who follow the lead of the church in the ensuing decade will hold fast to the principle of nonviolent civil disobedience.

Jean has come to this troubled land to join a mission team recruited from her diocese in Cleveland, Ohio. She leaves behind in the States her parents, her brother, close friends (including a special man in her life) and a career job with a prestigious accounting firm.

Both before and after she decides to join the mission team, Jean questions why God has chosen her to make a commitment so far removed from anything she's ever known before. The only answer the twenty-six-year-old woman gets is a deep-down sense that she's made the right choice.

Jean's soul-searching over Christian commitment started in college when she spent her junior year as a foreign exchange student at the University of Cork in Ireland. There she met a priest, Father Michael Crowley, who had recently returned from missionary work in Peru. He motivated her to volunteer in a Legion of Mary program of visiting the sick and helping the poor in Cork.

Jean returned home, first to graduate, then to earn a master's degree in business. After that she accepted a job with a national firm in Cleveland. Despite the advantages she enjoyed in her rising career, something seemed to be missing. After winning a trip to Europe at an office party, Jean made a return visit to Ireland in January 1977 to talk with her friend, Father Crowley, about the direction of her life. He advised, "You've got everything. You should think about giving a little back to God."[1]

Back in Cleveland Jean devoted her spare time to work in a diocesan program for inner-city youth, an environment considerably removed from her own childhood home in an affluent district of Westport, Connecticut.

In the fall of 1977, in response to Jean's quest for still more to do, a priest mentioned another diocesan project, this one connected with missionary work in El Salvador. The Cleveland diocese had been providing help to El Salvador since the early 1970s, trying to fill the gap when Salvadoran priests were persecuted and driven out. The diocesan team of volunteers maintained a close working relationship with Maryknoll missionaries in the area.

According to her mother, Jean had talked to a parish priest about her desire to become a missionary after returning from that junior year in Cork. Nevertheless, when Jean's friends and relatives heard what she planned to do, most found the idea of her as a missionary to be at odds with the fun-loving, motorcycle-riding Jean they knew.

To become a lay missioner, Jean was told, one must first be accepted into a four-month training course given by the Maryknolls at their center in Ossining, New York, for these are the professionals in the field. And after that comes three months of intensive Spanish-language instruction in Guatemala. (The present orientation program lasts from twelve to fourteen weeks, and missioners going to Spanish-speaking countries usually study the language in Bolivia.)

Part of the application process included writing an autobiographical essay. In it Jean told of the individuals Christ had sent her way to clarify her vocation, and of a serious illness her older brother Michael had that made her realize "how precious life is." Describing two of the most important influences, she wrote: "At times I'm sure my parents both wonder where I got the mission calling. To me it's obvious after having two people such as my parents to grow up with. My father is a gentle man. He has never been afraid to show love. I think I admire this about him best.... My mother is a very get up and go person who always seems to have the energy to do something for someone else."[2] (At one time, Pat had taught at a mission school in Dallas, and later worked with orphans through Catholic Charities in New York.)

In 1978, along with eight others, Jean was accepted into the course, which extended over the winter and into the spring of 1979. In May she went to Guatemala for Spanish school.

Her first close friend when she joins the team in August will be Ursuline Sister Dorothy Kazel, who has already been in El Salvador for some time. Jean's business background is immediately put to use: She is given charge of the mission accounts. As her first major assignment, she helps in the administration of a food distribution program for a community called Santa Cruz, near the airport. Evenings are given over to coordinating services for the peasants living there—men, women and young children. After laboring from dawn to dusk in the cotton fields of wealthy landowners, they have a supper of beans and tortillas, then go to "church," a wooden shack, where the Bible is read and discussed: the celebration of the Word. Jean experiences unexpected happiness at seeing that she can make a difference in the hard lives of the Salvadorans.

In her first months of work the political situation worsens, violence increases and, with civil war in sight, church workers begin making plans for refugee centers.

Spearheading the efforts of the Salvadoran church is

Archbishop Oscar Romero. When appointed to the episcopacy in early 1977 at the age of fifty-nine, Romero bore the image of conservative, a choice welcomed by the ruling class. Yet before long his sermons at Sunday morning Mass in San Salvador's cathedral were being applauded in church by the crowds of peasants attending. (The sermons were also broadcast to a larger audience.) When Jean is able to get to the capital, fifteen miles from her base, she, too, applauds Romero's preaching.

Though by nature shy, the archbishop feels called to speak out, to take a prophetic stance: "One who is committed to the poor must risk the same fate as the poor. And in El Salvador we know what the fate of the poor signifies: to disappear, to be tortured, to be captive, and to be found dead."[3]

Leaders of the bloodless military coup in mid-October 1979 promise democratic reforms, but the months that follow prove far from bloodless.

At Christmas Jean's parents, Ray and Pat Donovan, visit, wanting to see things for themselves and to meet their daughter's new friends. Pat remembers their first impression of El Salvador: "The most beautiful place we'd ever seen. Flowers covered the hills."[4] ("Where else would you find blooming roses in December?"[5] Jean had written in her diary.)

The overriding feeling everyone shares is that missionaries were not at risk, especially not Jean and her coworker Dorothy. Their blond hair and blue eyes identify them as North Americans. They will never be mistaken for Salvadorans as some of the missionaries with darker coloring may be. Any time an errand poses a safety problem, in fact, Jean and Dorothy are sent. No one has yet attacked a foreign woman, and there is no reason to think such an attack is likely.

In retrospect, Pat and her husband realize that Jean took them on the "back route," avoiding worrisome situations. An incident or two will come back to haunt them later, such as the time an armed, drunken soldier pushed his way into their van, demanding a ride somewhere. Jean and Dorothy quietly cautioned the parents: "Don't say a word."

As resistance groups scattered about the countryside prepare to fight against the violence of the National Guard and other government-sponsored forces, the mission team in La Libertad continues ministering to community needs. Determined to preserve an air of normalcy, they teach catechism, give instruction on health matters, dispense food and conduct religious services. Jean takes particular pleasure in organizing a church choir, even though she is teased about her musical abilities.

When her friend Doug Cable, a doctor she became acquainted with in Cleveland, comes to spend two weeks' vacation in early 1980, she shows him the beaches and other scenic attractions. Only afterward does he realize how, as with her parents' visit, Jean managed to keep him away from the trouble spots.

On March 24 church workers are stunned by the news that Archbishop Romero has been shot through the heart while celebrating Mass at the Convent of the Good Shepherd in San Salvador. Bomb blasts and bullets cause still more deaths during the funeral, which Jean attends.

A month later two Maryknoll nuns, Ita Ford and Carla Piette, arrive to work among the growing number of refugees, for the civil war is intensifying. They set up a refugee center in Chalatenango, a town in the mountainous northeastern province of the country, where guerrilla bands battle with government troops, forcing villagers to flee their homes.

When some of the people from her community of Santa Cruz are found hacked to death, Jean begins to fear for her own safety. The men of the La Libertad mission team add to their work burying the victims of death squads.

On a Sunday evening, July 6, Jean returns from the movies with two friends, young Salvadoran men, one the leader of her church choir. Jean parts company with them to go upstairs to her apartment above the parish school. Just as she reaches it, gunshots ring out. She rushes back down to the street, to the horrifying sight of both friends lying dead.

Though overwhelmed with grief—or because of it—Jean immerses herself in work. Sisters Ita and Carla can use all the help possible at their Maryknoll center in Chalatenango, for the welfare of refugees has become the paramount concern of the Salvadoran archdiocese. Jean and Dorothy start transporting peasants to refugee centers and other safe places as well as taking food and supplies where needed. One night in August, while the two Maryknoll nuns are on an errand of mercy themselves, they meet with an accident. Their jeep is caught up in a flash flood, and though Ita survives, Sister Carla drowns. Maryknoll sends Sister Maura Clarke as her replacement.

At this time, Jean and Dorothy find themselves working more closely than ever with the Chalatenango nuns. Their white Toyota van becomes a familiar sight as it traverses the countryside.

A few weeks after Carla's death, Jean's six-week vacation comes due. First she spends a few days with her parents, then goes on to London to meet Doug, and after that the two go to Ireland for a friend's wedding in Cork. During the days in Cork, Father Crowley as well as Doug try to convince Jean not to return to El Salvador. Others also try to dissuade her when she stops en route back at the Maryknoll Center in Ossining, for all can see that she is a basket case. But Jean keeps telling everyone she has to return, for she has promised the children in El Salvador she will. (Shortly before she died, Jean writes to a friend: "Several times I have decided to leave El Salvador. I almost could except for the children, the poor, bruised victims of this insanity. Who would care for them? Whose heart could be so staunch as to favor the reasonable thing in a sea of their tears and loneliness? Not mine, dear friend, not mine."[6]) One priest strongly advises her to think about it for three or four months before making a definite decision.

Jean spends several hours alone in the Maryknoll chapel on her last day there. When she comes out, the nun waiting to drive her to the airport describes her as completely changed from the way she went in, completely at peace with the decision to go back. Jean spends the final days of vacation in Florida with her parents. Jean tells them about the chapel incident: "God straightened the whole thing out for me." She only hopes God will keep her from being tortured. Otherwise, she's willing to die if necessary—then adds quickly that nothing is going to happen. ("She was the old Jeannie—happy," her mother says, remarking that her daughter was always a great one for talking to God like a friend.)

When Jean returns, her coworkers in El Salvador also note a marked change. Peaceful, confident, she is where she belongs.

Most of the last six weeks of her life are spent transporting people and supplies for the Chalatenango center. The church workers feel the pressure of surveillance. Threats are made, but still they feel their status as North Americans offers protection to the refugees in their care.

Unaccountably, the week before they die, Jean and Dorothy, who are both animal lovers, give away the dog and cat they have kept at their La Libertad apartment. Other than that, all seems normal.

The last weekend of November Ita and Maura leave for a four-day conference of Maryknoll Sisters in Nicaragua. Jean and Dorothy attend a reception at which they meet Robert White, the U.S. ambassador, and his wife, and accept an invitation to a dinner party at the San Salvador embassy on December 1. Worried about the women's safety driving after dark, the Whites insist they stay overnight.

On the afternoon of December 2, Jean and Dorothy make the five-mile drive to the airport to pick up two of the nuns returning from the conference in Nicaragua. They return to meet an early evening flight carrying Ita Ford and Maura Clarke. It is dark when the four leave the airport. They will never be seen alive again.

The following day Jean's parents receive notification that she is missing. On December 4 their worst fears are confirmed: Jean's body and those of her three coworkers are discovered in a ditch in a secluded spot. They have been sexually assaulted, then shot.

AFTERWARD

Two weeks before the killings, Ronald Reagan, president-elect at the time, sent emissaries to the Salvadoran government. They promised that, once Reagan became president, human rights violations would no longer be a factor in determining aid. The government would receive all the guns and other help it needed.

Despite protests from Ambassador White (who was soon the ex-ambassador), a cover-up persisted in shielding Salvadoran officials responsible for ordering the killings. Finally, in 1984, five National Guard soldiers were found guilty of the actual shooting.

Prior to the verdict, 19.4 million dollars had been frozen by the U.S. Congress, pending a resolution of the case. Within twenty-four hours of conviction, the U.S. State Department announced justice done, and released millions to the Minister of Defense, the very man who was commander of the National Guard at the time of the killings. In 1992 a formal peace treaty between the government and rebel factions was signed. And the following year a sweeping amnesty bill was passed by El Salvador's National Assembly.

Father Crowley of Cork was in the habit of telling his Legion of Mary group: "It's better to do something than to give up something." He would later say that Jean was the first to take him up on this. As her destiny would have it, however, in doing something, Jean gave up something, too: the ultimate, her life.

My Lord, my God,

Jean discovered
In a world so unlike her own,
The things that really mattered,
Like children, and roses in December
And the joy that comes from caring.

In counting my blessings—
Friends and family,
And awakening to a new day...
I make my thanksgiving.
Amen.

THE TWENTY-FIRST CENTURY

Dorothy Stang

Background

"Largest" defines many aspects of Brazil: in size, the largest country in Latin America; with a population nearing two hundred million, the largest number of Catholics (more than 80 percent) in any country of the world; and among its resources, the largest remaining rain forest on earth.

In a territory so vast—3.2 million square miles (almost the size of the United States)—paradoxically, the struggle over land continues to be a paramount issue, one in which the church today plays a role. (Less than 3 percent of the population owns two-thirds of the arable land.)

Problems initially surfaced back in the 1950s, with the introduction of agribusiness, or corporate-size farming, aided by mechanization, of course. Owing to this change in the way of doing things, millions of poor farmers were forced off their small plots.

Then came the coup of 1964, in which a democratically elected president was driven from power, and a military dictatorship took over (civilian rule not returning until 1985). After this happened, the Amazon region was opened up to speculators, foreign as well as domestic, who started clearing great tracts of rain forest to make space for ranches of massive size.

In the meantime, rising urban unemployment sent more of the population into rural areas. In a plan to resettle the economically displaced, the federal government began sponsoring a program in which grants of acreage in the northeast—the last frontier for the poor—were awarded. (Though a worthy plan on paper, the agency responsible for its implementation will perennially lack funding and other necessary resources.)

Not everyone was willing to welcome homesteaders with open arms, however; and, as a consequence, conflicts arose. It did not augur well for the voiceless poor.

Stepping in to protect the rights of peasant farmers and rural workers, and to push for land reform, Brazil's Conference of Catholic Bishops, in 1975, created its Pastoral Land Commission.

ANAPÚ, BRAZIL, JANUARY 2005

On a road near the town of Anapú, in northeastern Brazil, thieves intercept a car and begin giving the driver a beating to force him into submission. Another car not far behind, a battered Volkswagen, comes to an abrupt halt and a woman jumps out. Rushing to the aid of the victim, she shouts at the thieves with enough authority in her voice that they flee the scene.

Now she helps the severely wounded man into her car and takes him to a hospital, staying at his bedside to lend comfort until, unfortunately, he succumbs to his injuries. His brother, in later relating the story, is incredulous that the woman would help his family, "Even though we aren't Catholic." (Protestants, primarily Pentecostals, represent a religious minority in Brazil.)

He was referring to Sister Dorothy Stang, a missionary nun who has been ministering in Brazil for almost forty years. Born in Dayton, Ohio, in 1931, the fourth of nine children, her dream from an early age is to become a missionary one day. The dream is nurtured by parents whose interests include concern for the needs of people in other countries; and, closer to home, they instill in their sons and daughters a compassion for the poor. During Lent, for example, it is customary to save the pennies otherwise spent on candy, giving the money to those less fortunate.

In another family activity that will prove valuable years later in Dorothy's ministry, the backyard becomes a model of organic gardening. Composting and the dangers of pesticides are among the lessons filed away. (Her father knows what he is talking about, for he is a chemical engineer.)

In 1948 Dorothy enters the Cincinnati based province of an international congregation, the Sisters of Notre Dame de Namur. Professing her final vows in 1956, she becomes Sister Dorothy, having already begun teaching in elementary schools in Illinois and Arizona. The latter assignment gives her a heaven-sent opportunity, which she readily takes—the chance to volunteer on weekends in aid of migrant workers. From there to eventually engaging in ministry to landless rural workers in Brazil turns out to be a natural transition.

In 1966, her congregation heeds the call that had been put out by Pope John XXIII during Vatican II, asking religious communities and dioceses in the United States to send missionaries abroad, wherever the need is great. With four other members of her order, Sister Dorothy embarks for Brazil, starting the journey of a lifetime.

It is a critical juncture in the history of the country: two years into a dictatorship, and two years before the Latin American church declares its "Option for the Poor" at Medellín, Colombia.

Soon enough, the Sisters will realize how naïve they had been at first about the political situation. For the worst years occurred between 1968 and 1978, when more than 120 bishops, priests and nuns, and nearly three hundred layworkers were arrested, with many of them tortured. Seven clerics suffered death. In addition to censorship of church newspapers and radio stations, some were closed down. Standing tall, Brazil's bishops openly criticized the government while defending the rights of those oppressed.

In the meantime, nevertheless, the Notre Dame sisters head for northeastern Brazil, a region known as the poorest one in the country. Their destination is Coroata, in the state of Maranhao.

Once there Sister Dorothy quickly progresses from organizing Bible study groups to involvement in the daily lives of her people. She needs only to win the trust of the women before saying, "Let's start a school for the children." Looking after the welfare of the women and children always remains high on her list of concerns, and remedying their lack of education is a good start. After a bit, the men, too, are ready to join in the efforts, and soon Sister Dorothy is talking to them about farming—a subject she knows well from her childhood.

In the early 1970s some of the families decide to take up the government offer of titles to acreage in the neighboring state of Pará, in an area bordering the Amazon jungle and its rain forest. Sister Dorothy volunteers to accompany them. The ensuing years will become filled with the day-to-day problems—and joys—in shepherding settlers' families in their quest for a life that goes beyond mere survival.

As the first step in planning for a settlement, which may average four hundred or more families, Sister Dorothy organizes them into cooperatives—small Christian communities in which they not only pray and study the Bible together, but participate in projects such as workshops for women (hygiene and childcare among them), creation of schools and instruction in sustainable farming for the men.

Soil erosion is a particular problem in this part of the country. To counteract it, certain types of crops are found to be more suitable than others. In order to be wise stewards of the land, they must practice crop rotation, raising, for example, cacao, coffee, pepper, manioc and vegetables.

The spiritual side of community life requires nourishment, too, and Sister Dorothy conducts rituals of celebration with music and dancing to uplift them. Even at the end of a long workday, the people find time for worship. (A priest to celebrate Eucharist with any regularity is a rarity.)

According to the plan for sustainable development, each settlement is expected to farm 20 percent of the land, setting aside 80 percent for rain forest preservation. But not everyone in the region is keen to preserve the rain forest. Quite the opposite for the powerful loggers and ranchers who view the Amazon forest as their own domain. To maintain control, they dismiss the government documents given to settlers, and produce deeds of their own when intimidation to drive settlers away fails to have the desired effect. The deeds are, of course, fraudulent, arranged with the cooperation of corrupt local authorities, including judges and the police. For even if government at the federal level professes wanting its policy of land reform to succeed, the real decisions occur at the local level, which is hundreds of miles north of the nation's capital in Brasília.

Taking advantage of the distance, and lack of law enforcement, land barons ignore federal regulations, pursuing instead an agenda of their own. They accrue their wealth by raising cattle on a grand scale. (Some ranches that are owned by multinational corporations have been compared in size to small countries.)

21 : DOROTHY STANG

As huge tracts of forest are destroyed in order to create pastures for cattle-grazing, the now shadeless grassland is subject to
the punishing effects of the tropical sun. Where trees formerly
dropped needles and leaves that turned into mulch, revitalizing
the soil, erosion now sets in, grassland turns to weeds, tempera-
tures rise and rainfall lessens. After perhaps six to ten years,
ranchers seek new pastures, cutting deeper into the forest, and the
relentless cycle continues.

As for the loggers, they covet the expensive hardwoods—cedar
and mahogany—which are much in demand in the United States,
China and Europe. The state of Pará is the largest producer and
exporter of wood products in Brazil, with much of the timber
coming from illegal deforestation or protected areas of public
land. Pará, in addition, bears the dubious distinction of having
the country's highest rate of assassinations related to land disputes. These deaths are hardly ever investigated, and even more
rarely prosecuted.

The issue comes to the fore when, in 1977, in the Amazon's
northwest section, a trade union leader named Chico Mendes
begins organizing rubber tappers to protect their rights. Their
livelihood is being threatened by the heedless practices of ranchers and loggers that are on the way to decimating the rain forest.
Realizing that besides the human toll exacted, the Amazon's rich
biodiversity suffers, too, Mendes becomes a champion of the
environment—frequent death threats notwithstanding. (The
Amazon rain forest contains, as example, an estimated one-tenth
of the earth's plant and insect life.)

Mendes and his supporters gain international attention, for
the health of the rain forest is being scientifically linked to climate change. Rain forests play a crucial role in absorbing carbon
dioxide from the atmosphere; and as they shrink in size, global
warming increases. Some refer to the forests as the "lungs of the
world."

To show appreciation for his efforts, the United Nations bestows on Mendes an award for environmental protection (naming him to the Global 500 Roll of Honor) in 1987. The following year a rancher shoots him to death, sparking worldwide outrage. (The president of Brazil will later compare Sister Dorothy to Mendes.)

In 1992 the United Nations convenes its second Conference on Environment and Development—otherwise known as the Earth Summit. (The first one was held twenty years earlier in Stockholm, Sweden.) Hosted by Brazil, the international gathering meets in Rio de Janeiro from June 3–14. It draws delegates from 172 governments who consider the urgent problems in safeguarding the environment, as well as related socioeconomic development. Nongovernmental organizations, some twenty-four hundred represented, hold parallel forums of their own, which are attended by seventeen thousand. (Sister Dorothy is among the attendees, for she has come to recognize the interconnectedness between care of the planet and care of the poor.) The Earth Summit concludes with a blueprint for action to achieve sustainable development worldwide. Included are statements on climate change, forest principles and biological diversity.

In the aftermath, while conservation laws are passed at the federal level in Brazil, destruction of the rain forest continues unabated, as do conflicts over the land. Never one willing to back down, Sister Dorothy persists in reporting abuses to both local and national authorities. She explains to those who worry about her safety, that it is possible for her to speak out because she belongs to an international congregation of nuns, has church backing from the Pastoral Land Commission and, moreover, a record of long years of ministry in northeastern Brazil. Anyhow, she adds, it is not her personal safety that matters, but the well-being of her people.

When another Notre Dame sister, who formerly worked with Sister Dorothy, asks what keeps her going, the intrepid nun, upon reflection, answers: "I have learned that faith sustains you, and I have also learned that three things are difficult: one, as a woman to be taken seriously in the struggle for land reform; two, to stay faithful to believing that these small groups of poor farmers will prevail in organizing and carrying their own agenda forward; and three, to have the courage to give your life in the struggle for change."[1]

In the ongoing battle it is surely discouraging when loggers and ranchers illegally invade the land of farmers, burn their houses and destroy their crops. Over and over, Sister Dorothy asks city, state and national officials to protect the defenseless farmers, but nothing is done.

When these incidents occur, she handles them in the most practical way possible. With the aid of rural workers, she gathers up food, clothing and blankets to take to the settlement affected. After distributing the goods, Sister Dorothy typically tells the farmers, "You can sit here and cry, or you can get busy and start rebuilding." In short order, twenty or thirty men will step forward and do just that. She routinely stays until the job is done.

The year 2004 proves a particularly eventful one for her. Sister Dorothy becomes a naturalized citizen of her adopted country (while also retaining U.S. citizenship). In June, after her enemies make false charges, accusing her of inciting violence and supplying ammunition to the farmers, her congregation sends out a call to the international community, asking for letters of support. The response is overwhelming.

Sister Dorothy expresses gratitude for the backing of her order, and especially for its allowing her to remain in Brazil, doing what's closest to her heart.

She is further gratified when, in July, the state of Pará names her "Woman of the Year" for her human rights work in the Amazon. That summer she also goes on pilgrimage to France and Belgium, in connection with the two-hundredth anniversary of the founding of the Sisters of Notre Dame de Namur.

The year ends on another high note, when the prestigious Brazilian Bar Association names her "Humanitarian of the Year" for her dedication in helping rural workers live in dignity and justice. On hand for the occasion are two of her siblings, brother David and sister Marguerite, who have come to Brazil to see "Dot" honored. The event takes place on December 10 in Belém, capital city of Pará. The ceremony is preceded by a candlelight vigil in a park across from the building where senators, civic leaders and other invited dignitaries are gathering. Accompanying Sister Dorothy to the vigil are many of her own—peasants who, her brother David says, likely never set foot in such a grand building. But they do so on this evening, filling the auditorium.

Though the higher echelons of society are often told to "Hate Sister Dorothy," she does have some friends in these circles who warn her to be careful, for they know she is on a hit list. But she dismisses the idea. "They'll never kill a seventy-three-year-old woman," she tells them.

The earlier-mentioned incident in which Sister Dorothy had gone to the aid of a man attacked by thieves takes place about a month after the award ceremony in Belém. Then, in the first part of February, as the cycle of violence against settlers intensifies, she appeals again for their protection. Among those she meets to complain about death threats is Brazil's Human Rights Minister.

On February 11, in a last phone conversation with her brother David, now back in the United States, she must cut the call short because people are at the door, asking her to go with them to families whose houses and crops have been burned.

Later that same day, at the settlement, Sister Dorothy engages in an angry exchange of words with one of her antagonists, telling the man he is on the wrong piece of property, and she has government documents to prove it: He must get off the land. He leaves.

Early the next morning, she starts on her way to a meeting at the settlement called "Good Hope," accompanied by two rural workers. They walk only a short distance when two *pistoleros* (hired gunmen) appear. From the Bible she is carrying, Sister Dorothy begins reading the passage of the Beatitudes: "Blessed are the poor in spirit..." These are her last words as six shots fired at close range strike her in the head and chest. The terrified workers with her flee, but will later be witnesses to Sister Dorothy's final moments.

AFTERWARD

Those who ordered the killing surely thought they had silenced Sister Dorothy's voice forever. But others now spoke for her. Her concerns for the impoverished as well as preservation of the rain forest were being addressed now to a wider audience, an international one. For the world press, in reporting Sister Dorothy's murder, began paying greater attention than ever to the decimation of the rain forest and its effect on global warming. (More damaging evidence was provided by the Brazilian government's own statistics on the alarming rate of destruction in recent years.)

Days after the shooting, several members of the Pastoral Land Commission deplored the weak judicial system, remarking that convictions and sentencing in such situations were "lamentable." Later in the year, at its annual meeting, the Brazilian Bishops' Conference reiterated its commitment to "opt for the poor."

With the world spotlight on the case, arrests of the two gunmen came quickly. After their trial in December, 2005, they were convicted, then sentenced to long prison terms. (Those responsible for planning and ordering the killing were scheduled to be tried.) Until the gunmen's sentencing, figures show that in the past thirty years, more than seven hundred advocates of land protection had been killed. Out of all those incidents, only nine men were ever convicted.

When Sister Dorothy's brother came to Anapú to visit his sister's grave, Father Jose Amarro, also an advocate of land protection who had worked closely with her, told David: "Maybe she will accomplish with her blood what she could not fully accomplish during her life."[2]

Pope John Paul II had voiced thoughts along those lines when he issued his encyclical, *Tertio Millennio Adveniente* ("On the Coming of the Third Millennium"): "At the end of the second millennium, *the Church has once again become a Church of martyrs. The persecutions of believers—priests, Religious and laity—has caused a great sowing of martyrdom in different parts of the world.... This witness must not be forgotten.*"[3]

CREATOR GOD,

DOROTHY LET NO BARRIERS—
AGE, GENDER OR ANYTHING ELSE—
STAND IN THE WAY
OF HER CARING FOR THE EARTH,
OF CARING FOR HUMANITY.

IF ONLY MORE WOULD CARE
FOR THE EARTH AND HUMANITY.
SHOULD THAT "MORE"
INCLUDE ME?
AMEN.

CONCLUSION

This story of women in the church has taken us across the map from Christianity's origins in the Near East, to Europe, to the Western Hemisphere. Now we reach the Southern Hemisphere where, during the twenty-first century, a predicted two-thirds of Christendom will be represented by people of developing nations.

Looking at the last twenty-five years, among the visible changes we see fuller participation in ministry by laypersons, women as well as men—much as in apostolic times.

Also reminiscent of the early church, martyrs feature prominently. One may wonder what prompts an individual to give the ultimate—life itself—for the sake of belief. At least one answer may be found in the words of a notation in Dorothy Kazel's prayer book, discovered after the nun was martyred in El Salvador in 1980:

> You cannot understand how hard it is for one to be practical who hopes for tenderness behind every face.... Others can be impersonal, but not one who believes that he is on an eminently personal adventure.... Others can be sensible, but not one who knows in his heart how few things really matter. Others can be sober and restrained, but not one who is mad with the loveliness of life, and almost blind with its beauty.[1]

SELECTED BIBLIOGRAPHY

Armstrong, Regis J. and Ignatius Brady, trans. *Francis and Clare: The Complete Works*. Mahwah, N.J.: Paulist, 1982.

Bede's Ecclesiastical History of the English Nation. Introduction by David Knowles. New York: E.P. Dutton, 1965.

Carrigan, Ana. *Salvador Witness: The Life and Calling of Jean Donovan*. New York: Simon and Schuster, 1984.

Curtayne, Alice. *St. Brigid of Ireland*. New York: Sheed and Ward, 1954.

Deen, Edith. *Great Women of the Christian Faith*. New York: Harper, 1959.

De Robeck, Nesta. *St. Clare of Assisi*. Chicago: Franciscan Herald, 1980.

Ellsberg, Robert. *All Saints: Daily Reflections on Saints, Prophets and Witnesses for Our Time*. New York: Crossroad, 1997.

Eusebius. *The History of the Church from Christ to Constantine*. G.A. Williamson, trans. New York: Penguin, 1965.

Fatula, Mary Ann. *Catherine of Siena's Way*. Collegeville, Minn.: Michael Glazier, 1989.

Flinders, Carol Lee. *Enduring Grace: Living Portraits of Seven Women Mystics*. San Francisco: HarperSanFrancisco, 1993.

St. Gregory of Nyssa. *Ascetical Works* (Life of Macrina). Virginia Woods Callahan, trans. Washington, D.C.: The Catholic University of America Press, 1967.

Gryson, Roger. *The Ministry of Women in the Early Church*. Collegeville, Minn.: Liturgical, 1976.

Holum, Kenneth G. *Theodosian Empresses: Women and Imperial Domination in Late Antiquity*. Berkeley, Calif.: University of California Press, 1982.

Kelly, J.N.D. *The Oxford Dictionary of Popes*. Oxford: Oxford University Press, 1986.

Kittler, Glenn D. *The Woman God Loved: The Life of Blessed Anne-Marie Javouhey*. Garden City, N.Y.: Hanover, 1959.

Kuhns, Elizabeth. *The Habit: A History of the Clothing of Catholic Nuns*. New York: Doubleday, 2003.

Lernoux, Penny. *People of God: The Struggle for World Catholicism*. New York: Viking, 1989.

Maddocks, Fiona. *Hildegard of Bingen: The Woman of Her Age*. New York: Doubleday, 2001.

McGinley, Phyllis. *Saint-Watching*. New York: Image, 1974.

Medwick, Cathleen. *Teresa of Avila: The Progress of a Soul*. New York: Knopf, 1999.

Menzies, Lucy. *Mirrors of the Holy: Ten Studies in Sanctity*. Harrisburg, Penn.: Morehouse, 1928.

————. *St. Margaret: Queen of Scotland*. New York: E.P. Dutton, 1925.

Newman, Barbara. *Sister of Wisdom: St. Hildegard's Theology of the Feminine*. Berkeley, Calif.: University of California Press, 1987.

Oden, Amy, ed. *In Her Words: Women's Writings in the History of Christian Thought*. Nashville, Tenn.: Abingdon, 1994.

Peers, E. Allison, trans. *The Life of Teresa of Jesus: The Autobiography of St. Teresa of Avila*. New York: Image, 1960.

Ruether, Rosemary Radford, and Eleanor McLaughlin, eds. *Women of Spirit: Female Leadership in the Jewish and Christian Tradition*. New York: Simon & Schuster, 1979.

Salisbury, Joyce E. *Perpetua's Passion: The Death and Memory of a Young Roman Woman*. Oxford: Routledge, 1997.

Scherman, Katharine. *The Flowering of Ireland: Saints, Scholars and Kings*. Boston: Little, Brown, 1981.

Sherwood, Grace H. *The Oblates' Hundred and One Years*. New York: Macmillan, 1931.

Swidler, Leonard. *Biblical Affirmations of Women*. London: Westminster, 1979.

Talbot, C.H., trans. and ed. *The Anglo-Saxon Missionaries in Germany*. London: Purnell and Sons, 1954.

Underhill, Evelyn. *Mysticism: A Study in the Nature and Development of Man's Spiritual Consciousness*. New York: New American Library, 1974.

Undset, Sigrid. *Catherine of Siena*. Kate Austin-Lund, trans. New York: Sheed and Ward, 1954.

von Hügel, Baron Friedrich. *The Mystical Element of Religion as Studied in Saint Catherine of Genoa and Her Friends*. London: J.M. Dent, 1909.

Walsh, Michael, ed. *Butler's Lives of the Saints.* San Francisco: HarperSan-Francisco, 1991.

Wilson-Kastner, Patricia, et al. *A Lost Tradition: Women Writers of the Early Church.* Lanham, Md.: University Press of America, 1981.

Woodgate, M.V. *St. Louise de Marillac: Foundress of the Sisters of Charity.* St. Louis: B. Herder, 1942.

NOTES

Introduction

1. Leonardo Boff, *The Maternal Face of God: The Feminine and Its Religious Expressions*, Robert R. Barr and John W. Diercksmeier, trans. (San Francisco: Harper & Row, 1987), pp. 73–74.
2. E. Allison Peers, trans. *The Life of Teresa of Jesus: The Autobiography of Teresa of Avila* (New York: Doubleday, 1991), p. 328.

The Second Century: Perpetua of Carthage

1. Herbert Musurillo, trans., *The Acts of the Christian Martyrs* (Oxford: Oxford University Press, 1972), p. 109.
2. Musurillo, p. 113.
3. Musurillo, p. 113.
4. Musurillo, p. 115.
5. Musurillo, p. 119.
6. Musurillo, p. 127.
7. Musurillo, p. 129.
8. Musurillo, p. 129.
9. Musurillo, p. 131.

The Third Century: Apollonia of Alexandria

1. Eusebius, *The History of the Church from Christ to Constantine*, G.A. Williamson, trans. (New York: Penguin, 1965), p. 276.
2. Jean Daniélou and Henri Marrou, *The Christian Centuries, Volume One: The First Six Hundred Years*, Vincent Cronin, trans. (New York: McGraw-Hill, 1964), pp. 173–174.
3. Jean Daniélou, "The Ministry of Women in the Early Church," *La Maison-Dieu*, Glyn Simon, trans., 1961, pp. 21–22.
4. Daniélou, p. 22.
5. Eusebius, p. 337.

The Fourth Century: Macrina of Cappadocia

1. Gregory of Nyssa, *Ascetical Works*, Virginia Woods Callahan, trans. (Washington, D.C.: The Catholic University of America, 1967), p. 166.
2. Gregory of Nyssa, p. 166.

3. Gregory of Nyssa, p. 167.
4. Gregory of Nyssa, p. 176.
5. Gregory of Nyssa, p. 172.
6. Gregory of Nyssa, p. 163.
7. Gregory of Nyssa, p. 177.
8. Gregory of Nyssa, p. 178.
9. Gregory of Nyssa, p. 179.

The Fifth Century: Pulcheria of Constantinople
1. Eleanor Duckett, *Medieval Portraits from East and West* (Ann Arbor, Mich.: The University of Michigan, 1972), p. 166.

The Sixth Century: Brigid of Kildare
1. Katharine Scherman, *The Flowering of Ireland: Saints, Scholars and Kings* (Boston: Little, Brown, 1981), p. 115.
2. Giraldus Cambrensis, as quoted in Alice Curtayne, *St. Brigid of Ireland* (New York: Sheed & Ward, 1954), pp. 55–56.

The Seventh Century: Hilda of Whitby
1. *Bede's Ecclesiastical History of the English Nation* (London: Aldine, 1965), p. 202.
2. *Bede's Ecclesiastical History of the English Nation*, p. 203.
3. Charles W. Kennedy, trans., *The Caedmon Poems* (Gloucester, Mass.: Peter Smith, 1965), p. 3.
4. *Bede's Ecclesiastical History of the English Nation*, p. 146.
5. *Bede's Ecclesiastical History of the English Nation*, p. 204.

The Eighth Century: Lioba, Anglo-Saxon Missionary to Germany
1. As quoted in Eleanor Duckett, *The Wandering Saints* (New York: W.W. Norton, 1959), p. 225.
2. C. H. Talbot, ed., *The Anglo-Saxon Missionaries in Germany* (New York: Sheed & Ward, 1954), p. 99.
3. Phyllis McGinley, *Saint Watching* (Garden City, N.Y.: Image, 1974), p. 121.
4. Talbot, p. 219.
5. Talbot, p. 216.
6. As quoted in Duckett, p. 228.
7. Talbot, p. 223.

The Ninth Century: Ludmila of Bohemia
1. Herbert Thurston and Donald Attwater, eds., *Butler's Lives of the Saints* (New York: P. J. Kennedy & Sons, 1956), p. 664.

The Tenth Century: Adelaide, Empress of the Holy Roman Empire
1. Berchmans Bittle, *A Saint a Day* (Milwaukee: Bruce, 1958), p. 329.

The Eleventh Century: Margaret of Scotland
1. Lucy Menzies, *St. Margaret: Queen of Scotland* (New York: E.P. Dutton, 1925), p. 39.

2. Menzies, p. 62.
3. Menzies, p. 62.
4. Menzies, p. 130.
5. Menzies, p. 98.
6. Menzies, p. 115.
7. Menzies, p. 168.

The Twelfth Century: Hildegard of Bingen
1. Lucy Menzies, *Mirrors of the Holy: Ten Studies in Sanctity* (Milwaukee: Morehouse, 1928), p. 18.
2. Menzies, *Mirrors of the Holy*, p. 5.
3. As quoted in Fiona Maddocks, *Hildegard of Bingen: The Woman of Her Age* (New York: Doubleday, 2001), p. 76.
4. Menzies, *Mirrors of the Holy*, p. 12.
5. Sabina Flanagan, *Hildegard of Bingen, 1098–1179: A Visionary Life* (London: Routledge, 1989), p. 193.
6. Hildegard of Bingen, *Illuminations of Hildegard of Bingen* (Sante Fe, N.M.: Bear & Company), p. 16.
7. As quoted in the Introduction of *Illuminations of Hildegard of Bingen*, p. 9.

The Thirteenth Century: Clare of Assisi
1. As quoted in René-Charles Dhont, *Clare among Her Sisters* (St. Bonaventure, N.Y.: The Franciscan Institute, 1987), p. 15.
2. Regis J. Armstrong and Ignatius C. Brady, trans., *Francis and Clare: The Complete Works* (Mahwah, N.J.: Paulist, 1982), p. 211.
3. As quoted in Dhont, pp. 116–117.
4. As quoted in Dhont, pp. 83–84.
5. As quoted in Nesta de Robeck, *St. Clare of Assisi* (Chicago: Franciscan Herald, 1980), p. 81.
6. As quoted in Mary Seraphim, *Clare: Her Light and Her Song* (Chicago: Franciscan Herald, 1984), p. 301.
7. As quoted in Seraphim, p. 96.
8. As quoted in Seraphim, p. 389.
9. As quoted in Bernard McGinn, *The Flowering of Mysticism: Men and Women in the New Mysticism (1200–1350)* (New York: Crossroad, 1998), p. 69.
10. As quoted in Seraphim, p. 167.

The Fourteenth Century: Catherine of Siena
1. Sigrid Undset, *Catherine of Siena*, Kate Austin-Lund, trans. (New York: Sheed and Ward, 1954), p. 184.
2. Mary E. Giles, *The Feminist Mystic and Other Essays on Women and Spirituality* (New York: Crossroad, 1982), pp. 10–11.
3. As quoted in Carol Lee Flinders, *Enduring Grace: Living Portraits of Seven Women Mystics* (San Francisco: HarperSanFrancisco, 1993), p. 125.
4. As quoted in Undset, p. 241.

5. As quoted in Flinders, p. 126.
6. As quoted in Menzies, *Mirrors of the Holy,* p. 153.

The Fifteenth Century: Catherine of Genoa
1. As quoted in Menzies, *Mirrors of the Holy,* pp. 159–160.
2. As quoted in Evelyn Underhill, *Mysticism: A Study in the Nature and Development of Man's Spiritual Consciousness* (New York: New American Library, 1974), p. 441.
3. As quoted in Menzies, *Mirrors of the Holy,* p. 167.
4. As quoted in Friedrich von Hügel, *The Mystical Element of Religion as Studied in Saint Catherine of Genoa and Her Friends* (London: J.M. Dent, 1909), p. 163.
5. As quoted in Robert Ellsberg, *All Saints: Daily Reflections on Saints, Prophets, and Witnesses for Our Time* (New York: Crossroad, 1997), p. 402.
6. As quoted in Menzies, *Mirrors of the Holy,* p. 176.
7. Underhill, p. 441.

The Sixteenth Century: Teresa of Avila
1. E. Allison Peers, ed., *The Life of Teresa of Jesus: The Autobiography of St. Teresa of Jesus* (Garden City, N.Y.: Image, 1960), p. 75.
2. Peers, p. 109.
3. Peers, p. 115.
4. Peers, p. 305.
5. As quoted in Underhill, p. 283.
6. Peers, p. 345.
7. As quoted in McGinley, p. 19.
8. As quoted in Elliot Wright, *Holy Company: Christian Heroes and Heroines* (New York: Macmillan, 1980), p. 30.
9. McGinley, p. 101.

The Seventeenth Century: Louise de Marillac
1. "Five Stages in the Life of Saint Louise" Seton Provincialate Archivist, 26000 Altamont Rd., Los Altos Hills, CA 94022.
2. As quoted in Ellsberg, p. 119.
3. Vincent Regnault, *Saint Louise de Marillac: Servant of the Poor,* Louise Sullivan, trans. (Rockford, Ill.: TAN, 1983), p. 114.
4. M.V. Woodgate, *St. Louise de Marillac: Foundress of the Sisters of Charity* (New York: B. Herder, 1942), p. 169.

The Eighteenth Century: Anne Marie Javouhey
1. Glenn D. Kittler, *The Woman God Loved: The Life of Blessed Anne-Marie Javouhey* (Garden City, N.Y.: Hanover House, 1959), p. 69.
2. Kittler, p. 72.
3. Kittler, p. 58.
4. Kittler, pp. 93–94.
5. Kittler, p. 195.

NOTES

The Nineteenth Century: Elizabeth Lange
1. Maria M. Lannon, *Mother Mary Elizabeth Lange* (Washington, D.C.: The Josephine Pastoral Center, 1976), p. 21.
2. Grace H. Sherwood, *The Oblates' Hundred and One Years* (New York: Macmillan, 1931), pp. 22–23.
3. Sherwood, p. 24.
4. Sherwood, pp. 24–25.
5. Lannon, p. 11.
6. Lannon, p. 10.
7. Lannon, p. 10.
8. Sherwood, p. 69.
9. Sherwood, p. 35.
10. Lannon, p. 16.

The Twentieth Century: Jean Donovan
1. Joe Lynch, "Jean Donovan's Legacy to Her Parents," *Sojourners*, June 1987, p. 24.
2. Ana Carrigan, *Salvador Witness: The Life and Calling of Jean Donovan* (New York: Simon and Schuster, 1984), p. 67.
3. Ellsberg, p. 526.
4. Author interview with Pat Donovan, August 11, 1988.
5. Carrigan, p. 221.
6. Carrigan, p. 218.

The Twenty-First Century: Dorothy Stang
1. Arthur Jones, "Community celebrates martyred nun's work and vision" *National Catholic Reporter Online*, March 25, 2005, available at http://findarticles.com/p/articles/mi_m1141/is_21_41/ai_n13717109.
2. David Stang, "Martyred in the rain forest," *Maryknoll* July/August 2005.
3. Pope John Paul II, *Tertio Millennio Adveniente*, 37. Emphasis original.

Conclusion
1. Carrigan, p. 210.

INDEX

Aachen, 76
Abbasid dynasty, 80
Acts of the Apostles
  account of Peter's imprisonment, 6
  first Pentecost in, 5
"Acts of the Martyrs," 2, 23, 24
Adelaide (Holy Roman empress)
  children, 90
  crowning of, 90
  death of, 94
  imprisonment, 88
  marriage
    first, 88
    to Otto the Great, 88–89
  monasteries, founding, 90, 93
  peacemaking efforts of, 93
Advent, 100
agape, defined, 21
Age of Enlightenment, 170
Ahumada, Teresa de. See Teresa of Avila
Aidan
  death of, 65
  influence on English monasticism, 63
  regard for Hilda, 64
Alcantara, Peter of. See Peter of Alcantara
Alcuin
  English origin of, 69
  influence on Carolingian
    Renaissance, 69
Alexander VI, Pope, 147
Alexandria
  Catechetical School, 27
  as center of learning, 27
  culture of, 29
  John Mark in. See under John Mark
Alighieri, Dante, 129
Amarro, Jose, 213
Anglo-Saxon Chronicle, 62, 98
Annisa
  handwork at, 38
  monastic life at, 37, 40
  self-support of, 38

Antioch
  "Christian," source of term, 6
  and conversion of Gentiles, 6, 9
  Paul's preaching in, 6
Antony of Egypt, as "Father of
    Monasticism," 36
Anwander, Thaddeus, 183, 188, 189
Apollonia of Alexandria
  birth of, 27
  church honoring, 26
  death of, 26
Apollos of Alexandria, 12
apostolic age
  beliefs during, 17
  end of, 16
  simplicity of, 106
Arcadius (Roman emperor)
  father of Pulcheria, 42
  wife of. See Eudoxia
Arius
  banishment of, 33
  teachings of, 33
  Theodosius the Great on, 42
  Valens' views on, 39
asceticism
  in place of martyrdom, 32
  See also specific ascetics
Athansius, biography of Antony of
    Egypt, 36
Athenais. See Eudokia
Avignon, papacy at. See "Babylonian
    Captivity"

"Babylonian Captivity," 129–137
baptism, sacrament of
  adult, 32
  baptisteries, 29
  evolution of, 29
  infant, 32
Barnabas, missionary journeys with
    Paul, 6

Basil the Elder
 as father of Macrina of Cappadocia, 34
Basil the Younger
 as abbot of Annisa, 38
 Caesarea, school at, 37
 Macrina of Cappadocia, influence
  on, 37–38
Basilica of St. Euphemia, 48
Bastille, storming of, 171
Battle of Hastings, 98
Bede, on Hilda of Whitby, 64, 66
Bede's *Ecclesiastical History of the English
 People*, 64
Beguines, 120
Benedictine Rule, 73, 108
Berengar, 88, 90
Bernard of Clairvaux, 108
Bernardone, Francis. *See* Francis of
 Assisi
Birgitta of Sweden, 129
Black Death, 128, 131, 133
Boff, Leonardo, 2
Bohemia. *See* Ludmila of Bohemia
Boleslav, 84
Boniface, Saint
 Bischofsheim, 73
 and Lioba, 71. *See also* Lioba
 tomb of, 77
 women, attitude toward, 2
Boniface VIII, Pope, 128–129
Book of Kells, 56
Book of Kildare, 56
Borivoy, Duke, 80, 81, 82, 83
Brazil
 agribusiness in, 203, 207
 Catholics in, 203
 Conference of Catholic Bishops, 204
 deforestation in, 208
 Pastoral Land Commission, 204,
  209, 212
 soil erosion in, 207
Brigid of Kildare
 as abbess, 52, 54, 58
 childhood of, 52–53
 consecration of, 54
 devotion to God, 53
 emancipation of, 54
 father of. *See* Dubtach
 hospitality of, 58
 illness of, 53
 legacy of, 59
 marriage arrangements for, 53
 mother of. *See* Brocseach
 slavery of, 52, 53–54

 stories of, 58
Brocseach, 52
Brothers and Sisters of Penance, 126
bubonic plague. *See* Black Death
Byzantium. *See* Constantinople

Caedmon
 Hilda of Whitby's influence on, 66
Caesarea
 as trade center, 34
Cambrensis, Giraldus. *See* *Book of
 Kildare*
Canmore, Malcolm, 97, 98, 102
Carmelite order, 153, 156
Carolingian Renaissance, 77
Carroll, John, 181–182
Carthage
 synod of, 220, 225
 trade in, 17
Carthusians, 106
cathedral schools, 57–58
Catherine of Genoa
 ascetical practices of, 143
 family of, 145, 147
 illness of, 144
 marriage of, 140–142
 portrait of, 145
 on purgatory, 146
 Thobia, care for, 142, 144
 Underhill, Evelyn, on, 146
 visions of, 142, 146
Catherine of Siena
 devotions of, 131
 The Dialogue, 135–136, 137, 166
 as Doctor of the Church, 137
 Dominican Third Order, 132
 family of, 132, 133
 influence of, 137
 letters of, 133, 135
 visions of, 131
 vow of virginity, 132
Catholic Foreign Mission Society. *See*
 Maryknoll
Catholic Reformation, 158, 160
celibacy
 in place of martyrdom, 32
 See also specific celibates
Chalcedon, Council of. *See* Council of
 Chalcedon
Charlemagne, 76
 crowning of, 79
 empire building, 76
 successors of, 81
 wife of, 76

Christianity
  as scapegoat, 18, 31
  as "the Way," 7, 9
  break with Judaism, 14
  catechumenate during, 18, 27
  in Egypt, 18–19, 32, 50
  in North Africa, 17, 25–26
  Lord's Supper in, 8
  martyrdom in, 23–24. *See also specific martyrs*
  moral instruction of converts, 18, 27
  nonviolence in, 18
  persecutions, 5, 14, 17, 18, 20–23, 25, 27, 31
  role of deaconesses. *See* deaconesses
  roots in Jewish faith, 8, 9
  treatment of widows in, 11
  view of early Christians, 7
  women's role in, 10, 15
  See also house churches
Chrysaphius
  plot against Pulcheria of Constantinople, 46
Church of St. George, 84
Church of St. Vitus, 84
Cistercians, 106, 108
Clare of Assisi
  as abbess, 121
  Alexander IV, Pope, on, 126
  ascetical practices of, 122
  at San Damiano, 118, 119
  biography of, 121
  family of, 117, 118, 121
  manual work and, 121
  meeting with Francis, 117
  miracles of, 124
  Poor Ladies, 119, 120, 122
  poverty and, 119, 120, 123–124
  Rule of, 124, 125
  Testament of, 120
  tonsure of, 117, 118
Claudius (Roman emperor)
  ascent of, 6
  death of, 13
Clarke, Maura, 199, 200
Clement V, Pope, 130
Clement of Alexandria
  on pagan practices, 28
  on role of deaconesses, 39
Clement, Saint, 80
Clermont, Council of. *See* Council of Clermont
Clotilde, Queen, 61
Clovis, King, 61

Cluny
  Javouhey and, 174, 177, 179
  Mayeul, 91–92
  monastic reform and, 88, 91, 106
Conleth, 52
  as bishop, 52, 57
  as metalworker, 57
Conrad III, 113
consecrated virgins. *See* virgins, consecrated
Constance, Council of. *See* Council of Constance
Constantine (Roman emperor)
  baptism of, 33
  capital of empire moved under, 34
  first ecumenical council, 33
  freedom of worship under, 32
  mother of. *See* Helena
Constantinople
  break with Rome, 81, 104, 105, 129
  as capital of Eastern empire, 43
  Empress Irene of, 79
  Great Church of, 43
  influence of, 49, 50
  security of, 43
  conversos, 153. *See also* Judaism
Corinth
  Acrocorinth, 8
  architecture of, 7
  Isthmian Games at, 10
  mobile society of, 7
  Prisca and Aquila in. *See* Prisca the Evangelist
  trade in, 7
Council of Chalcedon (451)
  nature of Christ defined at, 48
  Pulcheria of Constantinople's role in, 48
Council of Clermont (1095), 106
Council of Constance (1417), 137
Council of Ephesus (431)
  banishment of Nestorius, 46
  Virgin Mary, decisions on, 46
Council of Ephesus (449)
  Chrysaphius and, 47
  Eutyches and, 47
  as "Robber Council," 47
Council of Trent (1542–1563), 156, 160
Counter-Reformation. *See* Catholic Reformation
Crowley, Michael, 194–195, 202
Crusades, 106, 117, 119, 139
Cuthburg, 71

Cyril, Saint
    death of, 81
    views on Nestorianism, 45
deaconesses
    Clement of Alexandria on, 30
    duties of, 29, 30
    in formation of female candidates,
        29
    relationship to order of widows, 29,
        30
    role, in early Christianity, 26, 29, 32
    virginity of, 36
deacons, 72–72
Decius (Roman emperor)
    persecution of Christians, 31
diaconate, female. See deaconesses
Diary of a Pilgrimage (Egeria), 41
Didache, 14
Diocletian (Roman emperor)
    persecution of Christians, 31
Dionysius of Alexandria, 26, 27
Disibod, Saint, 110–111
Donovan, Jean
    death of, 201
    education of, 194–195
    in El Salvador, 193, 196–201
    family of, 194, 196, 197–198
    in Ireland, 194, 195
    as lay missionary, 195
Drahomira, 83–84
Dubtach
    influence on Brigid, 58
    marriage arrangements for Brigid, 53
    social status of, 52
Dunfermline Abbey, 103

Eanswythe, 62
early Christian literature
    apology, 16–17
    New Testament. See New Testament
Earth Summit, 209
Easter
    date for, conflict surrounding, 67
Eccleston, Samuel, 182, 187–188
Edward the Confessor, King, 97, 98
Edwin, King. See also Hilda of Whitby
    baptism of, 62
    death of, 62
Egeria
    journeys of, 41
    writings of. See Diary of a Pilgrimage
Eleanor of Aquitaine, 113
Elfleda
    as abbess of Whitby, 68

care of Hilda for, 64
Elizabeth of Hungary, 126
Emmelia
    vision of, 35
Ephesus
    Council of. See Council of Ephesus
    Demetrius's campaign against
        Christians, 13
    difficulties for Christians in, 12–13
    Paul in, 11, 13
    Prisca and Aquila in, 11–12
    worship of Artemis in, 13
Ethelbert of Kent, King, 62
Eudokia
    conversion of, 44
    daughter of, 44–45, 46
    Jerusalem, retreat to, 47
    marriage to Theodosius II, 44
    Nestorius, support of, 45
    pilgrimage to Holy Land, 46
    Pulcheria of Constantinople, plot
        against, 46
Eudoxia
    enmity toward John Chrysostom, 43
Eugenius III, Pope, 106
eunuchs
    in Byzantine Empire, 46
    Chrysaphius. See Chrysaphius
Eusebius, 31
Eutyches
    as godfather to Chrysaphius, 47
    opposition to Nestorianism, 47
    support of Monophysitism, 47

Favarone, Clare di. See Clare of Assisi
Felicitas
    arrest of, 19
    child of, 21
    pregnancy of, 21
Fiesca, Catherine. See Catherine of
    Genoa
Finian, 58
First Eucharistic Prayer, 24
Firth of Forth, 97, 102
Flavian (patriarch)
    death of, 47
    deposition of, 47
    Eutyches, deposition of, 47
Florence, Italy, 129, 134, 139
Folkestone, 62
Ford, Ita, 198, 199, 200
Francis de Sales, 165–166
Francis of Assisi
    attitude toward women, 2

as deacon, 120
and Friars Minor, 120, 126
journey to Holy Land, 122
preaching of, 117
at San Damiano, 123
Franciscan order. *See* Clare of Assisi;
Francis of Assisi
Frederick Barbarossa, 113
Frederick II, 124, 125
French Revolution, 170–171. *See also*
Reign of Terror; Richelieu,
Cardinal
Frisia, 76
Fulda, 76, 77

Galatians, Letter to the, 10
Grace Cup, 99
Granada, conquest of, 150
Great Schism, 136–137
Gregory of Nyssa
as brother of Macrina of
Cappadocia, 34, 40
journey to Constantinople, 39
on Macrina of Cappadocia, 34, 38
marriage of, 37
ordination of, 38
writings of. *See* "The Life of St.
Macrina"; *On the Soul and the
Resurrection*
Gregory I, Pope, 62
Gregory VII, Pope, 105
Gregory IX, Pope, 123
Gregory XI, Pope, 130–132, 135
Guibert, 107

Hadrian V, Pope, 147
Heidenheim, 76
Helena (mother of Constantine), 34
Henry II, 113
Henry VIII, 150
Hilda of Whitby
as abbess, 64–65
baptism of, 62
childhood of, 62
death of, 68
Elfreda, care of, 64
at Paris convent, 63
Hildegard of Bingen
biography of, 107
birth of, 107
correspondence of, 111
death of, 114
feast of, 115
habit of, 112
illness of, 108–109

influence of, 137
interdict on, 113–114
John Paul II on, 115
medicine, interest in, 111
Ordo Virtutum, 110
as reformer, 107
Scito Vias Domini ("Scivias"), 109,
110
visions of, 109, 110, 113
vows of, 108
history, male perspective in, 1
Holy Roman Empire, 90, 92. *See also*
Otto the Great; Adelaide
house churches
of Chloe in Corinth, 12
communication between, 8
egalitarian atmosphere of, 9, 10
of Mary, mother of John Mark, 6
of Prisca. *See* Prisca the Evangelist,
house church of
spread of, 6
Hroswitha, 89–90
Hundred Years' War, 131
Huneberc, 76

icons, veneration of, 70–71
indulgences, sale of, 149
Innocent III, Pope, 116
Innocent IV, Pope, 147
Inquisition. *See* Spanish Inquisition
Ireland
Druidism in, 52–53, 57
Egyptian monks in, 52
first convent in, 54
Golden Age of, 59
Kildare. *See* Kildare
literature in, 55
missionaries of, 59
monastic settlements in, 53
Patrick's influence on, 52
political structure of, 57
social status of poets, 53
value for education in, 55
Viking raids on, 59
written language of, 55
Irenaeus of Lyon, 17
Ironside, Edmund, 97
Italian Renaissance, 139, 147

Jacopone da Todi, 142
Jaricot, Pauline, 179–180
Javouhey, Anne Marie
childhood of, 171
death of, 179
excommunication of, 178

family of, 172, 173, 176
in French Guiana, 177–178
in Senegal, 178, 179
and slavery, 176
teaching method of, 175
visions of, 175
Jeanne de Chantal, 165–166
Jerome
Bible translation of, 40–41
women's support of, 40–41
Jesuit order, 189
Jesus
example of loving service, 3
feelings toward women, 1, 2
two natures of, 48
John Chrysostom, Saint
burial of, 46
enemies of, 43
stripped of episcopacy, 43
John Mark
in Alexandria, 28
as author of second Gospel, 6
martyrdom of, 28
John, Saint (apostle), 16
John of the Cross, 156–157
John XXIII, Pope, 205
Josephites, 189
Joubert, James, 184, 186, 187
Judaism
as root of Christian faith. See
Christianity, Jewish roots of
persecutions, 18
resistance to Roman occupation, 14
women's role in, 9

Kazel, Dorothy, 196, 197, 214
Kildare
architecture of, 57
cathedral school of, 58
crafts at, 57
manuscripts, production of, at, 56
women, authority of, at, 59
Know-Nothings, 188–189

Lancaster, Joseph, 175
Lange, Elizabeth
birth of, 183
cause of, 190–191
death of, 189
discrimination and, 185, 186, 190
family of, 183, 187
Oblate Sisters of Providence, and, 185–186
as Sister Mary, 185

Lateran Palace, 91
Legion of Mary, 192–193, 194, 202
Lent, 94, 100
Leo the Great, Pope
definition of Christ's two natures, 48, 49
on Eutyches, 49
against Monophysitism, 47–48
on Pulcheria, 46, 48, 49
Leo III, Pope, 79
liberation theology, 193
Libussa, 80
Life of Jutta, 115
"The Life of St. Macrina" (Gregory of Nyssa), 34, 38
Lioba
biography of, 74–75
birth, 72
children of, 82
correspondence with Boniface, 71, 73
death of, 77
and Hildegard, 76
hospitality of, 74, 75
Louis XIV, 170
Louis Philippe, 179
Louise de Marillac
"Charities," of, 164
Daughters of Charity, 165–167, 168–169
family of, 162
hospice care and, 167–168
illness of, 162
La Couche and, 161–162
marriage of, 162–163
medicine, knowledge of, 164
organizational skills of, 161–162
son of, 163, 168
Vincent de Paul, and, 161, 163–164, 168
love
as motivating force, 3
and service, 3
Loyola College, 189
Ludmila of Bohemia
first church in Bohemia, 80
martyrdom of, 83
residence in Prague, 80, 82
Luther, Martin, 149, 150

Macrina of Cappadocia
arranged marriage of, 34
community at Annisa. See Annisa
death of, 40

mother of. *See* Emmelia
renunciation of wealth, 38
siblings of, 35, 36. *See also* Gregory
of Nyssa
virginity of, 34–35
Macrina the Elder, 40
Magyars, 81–82, 90, 96
Mantellate. See Dominican Third Order
under Catherine of Siena
Marabotto, Cattaneo, 144–145
Margaret of Scotland
birth, 97
children of, 102
exile of, 97–98
Gospel Book of, 100
St. Margaret's Blessing, 99
St. Margaret's Stone, 103
Mark, Saint (evangelist). *See* John Mark
Martel, Charles, 70
martyrdom
in *Tertio Millennio Adventiente*, 213
substitutes for, 32
See also specific martyrs
"The Martyrdom of Saints Perpetua
and Felicitas," 23
Mary, Virgin. *See* Virgin Mary
Maryknoll, 192, 193, 199
Mendes, Chico, 208–209
Methodius, Saint, 81, 82
monasticism.
at Annisa. *See* Annisa
Celtic versus Roman, 67–68
in England, 64
and hospitality, 74, 75
in Ireland, 54, 59
reform of. *See* monastic reform *under*
Cluny
self-supporting, 54–55. *See also*
Annisa
social welfare and, 40
spread of, 77
for women, 32
work and, 75
See also specific monasteries
Monophysitism, defined, 47
Moors. *See* Muslims
Moravia, 81
Muslims
in Europe, 88, 92
Islamic culture, 139
Moors, 150
in North Africa, 70

Napoleon, 172

Naseau, Marguerite, 164–165
Nero (Roman emperor)
ascent to power, 13
persecution of Christians, 14, 17
reputation of, 13
Nestorius
Virgin Mary, views on, 45
New Testament
contents of, 16
order of widows in, 36
Nicaea, Council of
Arianism and, 33
formulation of Nicene Creed, 33
Nicene Creed
formulation of, 33
Norman Conquest, 98
Notre Dame, cathedral of, 106

Oblate Sisters of Providence, 182. *See
also* Lange, Elizabeth
Odilo, 89, 93, 94
Odoacer, 49
Olga of Kiev, 105
On the Soul and the Resurrection
(Gregory of Nyssa), 39
Opus Angelicum, 99
Origen, 27
Oswald, King, 63
Oswy, King
Celtic traditions of, 67–68
daughter of. *See* Elfleda
defeat of pagans, 64, 66
gift of land to Hilda of Whitby, 64
Otto II, 91, 92
Otto the Great
death of, 90–91
defeat of Magyars, 96
as Holy Roman Emperor, 90
rule of, 84, 88
Otto the Pious. *See* Otto the Great
Ottonian Renaissance, 89, 94

Pachomius
community aspect of monasticism
and, 36
Mary, sister of, 36
paganism, 72
papacy
authority of, 112
at Avignon. *See* "Babylonian
Captivity"
political influence of, 105, 128
primacy of Roman see, 68
spiritual leadership of, 91

See also specific popes; Papal States
Papal States, 124, 130
patriarchates
rivalry among, 49
See also specific patriarchates
Patrick, Saint
childhood of, 51
influence on Ireland, 51–52, 55
study in France, 51
Paul, Saint
attitude toward women, 2, 10
baptism of Lydia, 10
Corinthians, First Letter to the, 12
Galatians, Letter to the, 10
missionary journeys
to Corinth, 12
to Cyprus, 6
to Ephesus, 11
to Jerusalem, 11
opposition to, 9, 11, 13
Phoebe, trust in, 10
preaching in Antioch, 6, 8–9, 11
Romans, Letter to the, 13–14
trade as tent-maker, 9
Paulinus
baptism of Edwin, 62
baptism of Hilda, 62
as escort to royal family, 63
Paul of Ancona, 82
Peace of Constantine, 37
Perpetua of Carthage
arrest, 19
birth, 17, 27
brother of, 22
child of, 19, 20
conversion, 17–18
diary of, 19, 23–24
father of, 20
in First Eucharistic Prayer, 24
instructor of. *See* Saturus
marital status of, 20
martyrdom of, 22–23
Tertullian on, 23
trial of, 20
visions of, 20
Peter, Saint
imprisonment of, 6
preaching at first Pentecost, 5
preaching in Rome, 12
preeminence of, 68
Peter of Alcantara, 154, 155
Peter's Pence, 116
Philip II, 157
Philip IV, 128

Piette, Carla, 198, 199
pilgrimages
in Europe, 91
origin of, 34
Pius II, Pope, 140
Pius VII, Pope, 174
priesthood
celibacy and, 38
ministry of, 32
Prisca the Evangelist
Apollos of Alexandria, instruction of, 12, 14
Church of St. Prisca, 14
house church of, 13, 14
John Chrysostom on, 14
Letter to the Hebrews, as author of, 14
marriage of, 7
in Paul, writings of, 13
Pudens, Senator, relationship to 6–7
Tertullian on, 14
trade as tent-maker, 7–8
Protestant Reformation, 156. *See also* Luther, Martin
Pulcheria of Constantinople
ascetical practices of, 44
as consecrated virgin, 44
death of, 49
Gibbon on, 44
John Chrysostom, burial of, 46
legacy of, 49
marriage to Marcian, 48
Nestorianism, views on, 45–46
plot against, 46–47
regency of, 43–44
as Roman empress, 48
vow of virginity, 44, 48
purgatory, 146, 149

Radegund, Queen, 62
Raymond of Capua, 134, 136, 137
Reformation. *See* Protestant Reformation
Reign of Terror, 172
Revolution of 1848, 179
Richardis of Stade, 111
Richelieu, Cardinal, 160
"Robber Council." *See* Council of Ephesus (449)
Roman Empire
Christians in, 5
end of, 49
Germanic invasions of, 43, 48, 49

persecutions in, 5, 14. *See also* persecutions *under* Christianity
Ravenna, Western capital at, 43
split into East and West, 43
Romero, Oscar, 196–197, 198
Rupert, Saint, 110–111
sale of indulgences. *See* indulgences, sale of
Saracens. *See* Muslims
Saturus
diary of, 20–21
martyrdom of, 22–23
visions of, 21
Scillium (Carthage), martyrs of, 17
Second Vatican Council. *See* Vatican II
Secundulus, death of, 21
Septimius Severus (Roman emperor)
North African origins, 17
persecution of Christians, 18, 25, 27
Seton, Elizabeth, 186, 190
Sisters of Charity, 186
Sisters of Notre Dame de Namur, 205. *See also* Stang, Dorothy
Society for the Propagation of the Faith, 179–180
Spanish Inquisition, 153
St. Margaret's Blessing, 98
St. Margaret's Stone, 103
Stang, Dorothy
birth of, 205
citizenship of, 210
cooperatives, organizing, 206–207
death of, 212
family of, 205, 211
gardening, interest in, 205
"Humanitarian of the Year," 211
opposition to, 211
ritual celebrations of, 207
Sulpician Society, 188
Sylvester II, Pope, 96

Tabennisi, 36–37
table fellowship *See* Christianity, Lord's Supper in; agape
"Teaching of the Twelve Apostles." *See* Didache
temple of Jerusalem, destruction of, 14
temple prostitution, 12
Teresa of Avila
at Convent of the Incarnation, 151, 152–153
devotion to Saint Joseph, 152
as Doctor of the Church, 137, 159
family of, 150, 151, 152, 154–155

illness of, 151–152
The Interior Castle, 157
love for Jesus, 3
opposition to, 154–155
Primitive Rule and, 153–156
sense of humor, 157–158
Spanish Inquisition and, 153, 157
travels of, 158
visions of, 154
The Way of Perfection, 156
Tertullian, on martyrdom, 24
Theodora (empress), 71
Theodosian Code of Law, 46
Theodosius II (Roman emperor)
death of, 48
Eudokia, marriage to, 44, 46
Nestorian controversy and, 45
Pulcheria's regency of, 44
and "Robber Council," 47
Theodosius the Great (Roman emperor)
on Arianism, 42
penance of, 42
Pulcheria, granddaughter of, 43. *See also* Pulcheria of Constantinople
on women, 42
Theophano, 92, 93
Therese of Lisieux, 137
Third Spiritual Alphabet (Francisco de Osuna), 152
Thirty Years' War, 167
Thomas Becket, 113
Thomas of Celano, 121, 125
tonsure
Celtic versus Roman, 67–68
of Clare of Assisi. *See* Clare of Assisi
Trent, Council of. *See* Council of Trent
"Truce of God," 94
Turgot, 99–100, 103

United States Catholic Almanac, 187
Urban II, Pope, 106
Urban V, Pope, 129
Urban VI, Pope, 135, 136

Valens (Roman emperor)
Gregory of Nyssa, opposition to, 39
pro-Arianism of, 39
Vatican II, 161, 205
"Velvet Revolution," 85
Vernazza, Ettore, 144, 145
Victor (Roman emperor), 17
Villanova University, 190
Vincent de Paul, 2, 161. *See also* Louise de Marillac, Vincent de Paul and

Virgin Mary
  as "Mother of God," 46
  Nestorian controversy over, 45–46
  veneration of, 106
virgins, consecrated
  dress of, 36
  in Ireland, 54
  in order of widows, 36
  practices of, 36
Volmar, 111

Ward, Mary, 166
Wenceslaus, 81, 83, 84, 85
Whitby. *See also* Hilda of Whitby
  acquisition of land for, 64
  library at, 65
  manuscript production at, 65
  music at, 65
White, Robert, 200–201
widows
  in Dominican Third Order, 132
  in early Christian society, 11–12
  order of, 29, 30, 36

Willibald, 76
Willigis, 93
Wimborne Abbey, 72, 73–74
women
  in Anglo-Saxon society, 68
  attraction of convent life for, 38
  authority of, at Kildare, 59
  Jesus' feelings toward, 1, 2
  ministry of. *See* widows, order of;
    deaconesses
  religious communities. *See specific*
    orders
  Resurrection, first witnesses of, 1
  rules for religious life, 125
  Scripture study and, 41, 56, 75, 99,
    206

Zacharias, Pope, 72